20th Century Defences in Norfolk

Mike Osborne
with Alistair Graham Kerr

CONCRETE PUBLICATIONS

Published by Concrete Publications
45 Church Street
Market Deeping
Lincolnshire
PE6 8AN

British Library Cataloguing in Publication Data;
A catalogue record is available from the British Library.

ISBN 978-0-9540378-3-3

Laid out by Andrea Nolan of Armadillo Design & Print, Northampton

Printed by Armadillo Design & Print, Northampton [01604 790763]

Dr Mike Osborne has lived on the borders of East Anglia since 1974. An early interest in mediaeval fortification extended into more recent periods, and he has written on English Civil War sieges and fortifications. He was a volunteer Area Co-ordinator for ten eastern counties, including Norfolk and Suffolk, for the Defence of Britain Project from 1995. His Defending Britain, an examination of 20th Century military structures in the British landscape, was published by Tempus in 2004, followed by Pillboxes in Britain and Ireland in 2008, also by Tempus. A recent project has been a survey of the 2500-odd drill halls and TA Centres in Britain, published by Partizan Press as Always Ready. He has been a member of the Fortress Study Group, the Airfield Research Group, and other similar groups for many years. This is his fifth book in this 20th Century Defences series, and the fourth to be published by Concrete Publications.

Alistair Graham Kerr, with family roots in both archaeology and the military, has spent many years researching aspects of fortifications especially those of the 20th Century. He worked at the centre of the Defence of Britain Project, and is a long-term member of the Pillbox Study Group, editing its journal Loopholes. He is an active member of the Fortress Study Group involved in organising its conferences. He cares for much of the archive material belonging to both groups. He lives and works on the borders of Suffolk and Norfolk.

Front cover illustration:
Shell-proof pillbox on Pophams Eau at Nordelph [TF552009]

Opposite Page:
The Fort-style watch office at Bircham Newton

CONTENTS

ACKNOWLEDGEMENTS

Adrian Armishaw, Derek Bales of Stoke Holy Cross, Christopher Bird, Peter Kent, the Muckleburgh Collection, Norman Nicol, Andrea Nolan for origination, Simon Purcell, Eric Rhodes, Doug Robb of Neatishead, Neil Storey, Tony Thurlow of Syfer, Ray Towler, the staff at the TA Centre in Aylsham Road, Norwich.

PICTURE CREDITS: all illustrations are Mike Osborne's unless otherwise indicated;

ABBREVIATIONS

AA	Anti-aircraft
AAOR	Anti-Aircraft Operations Room [ROTOR system]
AAP	Aircraft Acceptance Park
AAP	Advanced Ammunition Park
ADGB	Air Defence of Great Britain [1924 scheme]
AEW	Airborne Early Warning [usually Boeing Sentries]
AFV	armoured fighting vehicle
AMES	Air Ministry Experimental Station [original CH radar stations]
ARG	Airfield Research Group
ARP	Air Raid Precautions
ARS	Aircraft Repair Shed
ASC	Army Service Corps [Royal from 1918]
AT	anti-tank
AVRE	Armoured Vehicle Royal Engineers
BEF	British Expeditionary Force
BL	breech-loading [gun]
Bn.	battalion
Bty.	battery
CASL	Coast Artillery Searchlight [WWII] see also 'DEL'
CBA	Council for British Archaeology
CD	Civil Defence
CD	Coast Defence [radar]
CH	Chain Home [radar]
cwt	hundredweight [51kg]
DEL	Defence Electric Light [WWI searchlight] see also 'CASL'
DEMS	Defensive Equipping of Merchant Ships
EFTS	Elementary Flying Training School
EH	English Heritage
FAA	Fleet Air Arm [formerly RNAS qv]
FAD	Forward Ammunition Depot

FFMT	Fire-fighting Motor-transport [ready-use on airfields]
FTS	Flying Training School
FIDO	Fog investigation & dispersal organisation
GCI	Ground-Controlled Interception [radar system]
GDA	gun-defended area
GHQ	General Headquarters [as in GHQ Line]
GL	gun-laying [as in radar for AA artillery]
GOR	Gun Operations Room [AA in WWII]
GPO	General Post Office
GR	Georgius Rex [royal cipher]
GS	General Service [as in WWI Belfast Truss hangar]
HAA	Heavy Anti-aircraft
HG	Home Guard
hp	horse-power
HSL	High-speed Launch [RAF air/sea rescue]
IRBM	Intermediate Range Ballistic Missile [THOR]
ITC	Infantry Training Centre
LAA	Light Anti-aircraft
LDV	Local Defence Volunteers
lmg	light machine-gun
LNER	London North Eastern Railway
MAFF	Ministry of Agriculture, Fisheries & Food
MAP	Ministry of Aircraft Production
MCU	Marine Craft Unit [RAF]
MFV	Motor Fishing Vessel [RN]
MGB	Motor Gun-boat [RN]
ML	Motor-launch [RN]
MMS	Motor Minesweeper [RN]
MTB	Motor Torpedo-boat [RN]
MT	Motor Transport
MoD	Ministry of Defence

MOW	Ministry of Works
MOWP	Ministry of War Production
mph	miles-per-hour [5mph=8kmph]
m/s	Mine-sweeper/sweeping
MU	Maintenance Unit [RAF]
NFE	Night-Flying Equipment [Store on airfields]
OB	Operational base [Auxiliary units]
OP	Observation Post
OTU	Operational Training Unit [RAF]
PBX	private telephone exchange as found on airfields
pdr.	pounder [as in weight of projectile] 1 pound = 454grams
pers com[s]	personal communication[s]
PH	public house
PIAT	Projector Infantry Anti-Tank
PLA	Port of London Authority [responsible for marine salvage]
PWSS	Port War Signal Station
PoW	Prisoner of War
QF	Quick-firing [gun]
RDF	Radio Direction-finding
RAF	Royal Air Force [from 1 April 1918]
RAOC	Royal Army Ordnance Corps
RASC	Royal [from 1918] Army Service Corps
RCHME	Royal Commission on Historical Monuments [England]
Regt.	Regiment
REME	Royal Electrical & Mechanical Engineers
RE	Royal Engineers
RFC	Royal Flying Corps [up to 31 March 1918]
RGA	Royal Garrison Artillery
RLG	Relief Landing Ground
RM	Royal Marine
RML	Rescue Motor-launch [RN air/sea rescue boat]

RN	Royal Navy
RNAS	Royal Naval Air Service [later Fleet Air Arm]
RNVR	Royal Naval Volunteer Reserve
ROC	Royal [from 1941] Observer Corps
ROF	Royal Ordnance Factory
RSG	Regional Seat of Government
RTR	Royal Tank Regiment
SAA	Small arms ammunition
SAC	Strategic Air Command [USAF]
SAF	Strategic Air Force [US]
SAM	Surface-to-air missile
SIS	Secret Intelligence Service
S/L	searchlight
SLG	Satellite Landing Ground
SOE	Special Operations Executive
SSSI	Site of Special Scientific Interest
Sub-RSG	sub-Regional Seat of Government
TA	Territorial Army [from 1920]
TAC	Territorial Army Centre [drill hall post-1947]
TAF	Tactical Air Force [US]
tb	temporary brick [single brick with buttresses in RAF buildings]
TF	Territorial Force [from 1908-1918]
UEA	University of East Anglia
UKRAOC	United Kingdom Regional Air Operations Centre
UKWMO	United Kingdom Warning & Monitoring Organisation
UP	un-rotated projectile [as in Z battery, AA rockets]
USAAF	United States Army Air Force [throughout WWII]
USAF	United States Air Force [after WWII]
WRAF	Women's Royal Air Force
WRNS	Women's Royal Naval Service [Wrens]

INTRODUCTION

Norfolk may have sometimes been referred to, rather unkindly, as a back-water but during the 20th Century's two world wars it was in the front-line of both the naval and aerial struggles, and would, quite probably, have been at the fore-front of the land war, had the enemy carried out his intention to invade. Despite being spared this last, the county nevertheless witnessed the full effect of what had come to be described as Total War. A majority of the population found itself in uniform, women as well as men, many of these in a patriotic response to the nation's plight, but many more through conscription and with very little choice. Youngsters could no more avoid the perils and excitements of the situation than could their parents. Boy Scouts carried out coast-watching duties in World War I, schoolboys served in the Home Guard in World War II, and those too young to be called up found ways to enlist in both wars. Young girls assumed early domestic responsibility for younger siblings or evacuees or casualties or simply the eternal quest for food, fuel and everyday commodities. Civilians were in the firing-line from coastal bombardment, from aerial bombing or from accidents caused by the black-out, or by unfamiliar work. Shortages of food, clothes and shelter hit everyone, though, as ever, some more than others. The war economy dominated industry and agriculture, requiring people to learn new skills, and to adapt to new circumstances. Even the very landscape changed. The coast was fortified, the beaches sealed off with barbed-wire, mines and obstacles and the local population excluded. Every scrap of arable land went under the plough, flower gardens being replaced by vegetable plots. Feltwell Fen, for instance, was singled out by the Ministry of Information as a case-study of a success story. Here, 1500 acres [600 hectares] of land was reclaimed from waste. Organised by the Norfolk CWAEC [County War Agricultural Executive Committee], a combined effort of the local farmers, land girls, military earth-moving equipment, and the REs blasting the bog-oaks of submerged petrified forests, managed to drain the marshes, to lay concrete roads, and thus enable the rich earth to produce first-class harvests. Much land was swallowed up for military camps, airfields and training grounds, and town and country houses requisitioned for hospitals, for military camps, and for PoW camps. Large areas around Thetford, taken over as the Stanford Battle Area, have still never been returned to their former occupants. Private vehicles were commandeered or immobilised, and roads punctuated by check-points and road-blocks. Nobody could say they didn't know there was a war on, and few were spared heartbreak, discomfort or pain.

Whilst much of the evidence on the ground for all this has long disappeared, a great deal still remains. Given that tourism lies at the heart of the coastal economy it was inevitable that the County Council should seek to remove the reminders of war as fast as possible. In 1945, a schedule of works to demolish pillboxes, anti-landing obstacles and coast artillery batteries was drawn up on the basis of three categories of priority. Despite this, many of the defensive works still remain, but are now suffering more from the coast's natural erosion than conscious attempts to destroy them by human agency. When Christopher Bird, Peter Kent, Simon Purcell and Mike Osborne carried out a county-wide survey of 20th Century defences in the mid-1990s, much more survived than is now the case, and despite recent information from Christopher that storms have temporarily uncovered the shattered remains of Cley Battery, blown up in 1955, the process is inexorably one-way. Airfields too are fast disappearing. The insatiable thirst for brown-field sites, along with the essentially ephemeral nature of most military buildings, and the benefits of the peace dividend, means that airfields are being transformed into housing estates with the flying-fields often being returned to agriculture. The hunger for housing appears to predominate, but there is no shortage of demands for land: if not a housing estate then, perhaps a prison as may be built at Coltishall, or an industrial training centre as at Bircham Newton. This process is inevitable, one would not wish it otherwise, and there is only room for so many museums, but we are moving very rapidly from a state of having a great number and variety of modern military monument to the opposite. We stopped demolishing castles some time ago partly because they informed us about our history: social, political, military and architectural. We cannot afford to lose an entire slice of 20th Century history merely because airfields and pillboxes tick fewer boxes in the romantic or aesthetic domains.

This book sets out to describe the modern military landscape of Norfolk, illustrating it from currently surviving examples of structures. It is one of a series, begun by Brasseys, and since continued by Concrete Publications, and which originated in the Defence of Britain Project. That Project, was organised by the Council for British Archaeology, ran from 1995-2002, and sought to log the thousands of military sites representing the full range of 20th Century military history. The general public was encouraged to identify such sites and to record them on pro-formas for posterity. Tens of thousands of completed forms were collected demonstrating both the interest and enthusiasm for the topic, and the wealth of material surviving. No doubt there are still survivals to be rediscovered, by the same process through which lost mediaeval city walls, or Roman floors reappear after many centuries of concealment. Readers who might seek to make such discoveries are asked to observe three principles: to respect private property and privacy; to take appropriate care in potentially hazardous locations; and to report discoveries to local authority sites and monuments officers or to local museum staff.

Mike Osborne & Alistair Graham Kerr
August 2008

ANTI-INVASION DEFENCES IN NORFOLK 1

From time immemorial, it had been mainly the south coast of Britain that lived with the threat of foreign invasion until, that is, around 1905. Apart from a few Dutch adventures around the Thames Estuary and Harwich in the Seventeenth Century, and the strange events at Fishguard, in 1797, it was always the ports of the south that were actually attacked or threatened in any major war. However, as the German menace developed in the years preceding the outbreak of World War I, it became necessary to put in train plans to defend the east coast against an invasion from across the North Sea. For reasons of economy, tradition and a failure to think too deeply about it, the notion, a hang-over from Napoleonic times, that the Royal Navy would always protect the nation from invasion, maintained currency. Why, asked the politicians, go to the expense and trouble of building unnecessary fortifications along our coasts when the enemy would never get close enough to test them? In 1914, therefore, there were few fixed defences on the Norfolk coast or, for that matter, anywhere in East Anglia.

Anti-invasion defences in World War I

What little existed of Norfolk's fixed defences in 1914 were mainly a legacy from Victorian times, consisting of a single obsolete coast defence battery defending the port of Great Yarmouth, and a similarly ineffectual battery at Kings Lynn, built for the Coastguards to practise on. In short, the sophisticated Edwardian coast defences of the English south coast with their specialised Counter-Bombardment and Coast Defence Batteries were, apart from Harwich Haven, entirely missing from the shores of East Anglia. On the outbreak of war immediate steps were taken to defend the most obvious landing places on Norfolk's most vulnerable beaches. Trenches, supported by barbed-wire, were dug at Weybourne and at Sheringham, and some mobile batteries of the RGA, with 60 pounder howitzers, were stationed in suitable places, such as Weybourne and Mundesley, to be able to fire on potential invasion beaches. A bombardment of Great Yarmouth in the early months of the war by German warships caused little damage, but served as something of a wake-up call. A single 4.7 inch gun was emplaced on Gorleston Cliffs, two more at Cromer, and some 15 pounder guns at Salthouse [two], Eccles, Hemsby [actually at Newport] and at Caister. Unlike the south coast batteries with their massive concrete emplacements, these were quite weak, that at Gorleston consisting of a magazine linked to two sub-surface crew-shelters with the gun mounted on its hold-fast on an open platform. Many of the other guns were still on field carriages, making them more vulnerable, less effective and harder to lay accurately on moving targets. These were no more than light coast defence guns, and certainly no insurance against the future bombardments which inevitably came. On 25 April 1916 Great Yarmouth was again bombarded, resulting in four deaths; on 26 November 1916 an armed trawler was sunk off the town; and on 14 January 1918 a fourth visit from German warships saw 50-60 shells land, causing seven more deaths. In the context of the enormous casualty figures of World War I, these may have been tiny tragedies, but when the German battle-cruisers came calling, the targets were mainly defenceless civilians, and there was apparently nothing the forces could do to protect them.

The defensive strategy determined in the War Office was simple. The meagre defences on the coast, backed up by further fieldworks near Holt, were supported by a large force of troops, intended to be mobile enough to respond quickly to any enemy landing. In the early days, many of these troops were horsed Yeomanry. In early 1915, the 1st South Midlands Mounted Brigade, consisting of the Gloucestershire, Warwickshire and Worcestershire Yeomanries, along with the Warwickshire Royal Horse Artillery, had its HQ at Cumberland House, Hunstanton. Later that year these regiments had all left for Egypt and the Gallipoli expedition, but their duplicate, second-line units spent the war in East Anglia, converted into cyclist units, the Worcestershire Yeomanry being based at Holkham Hall, for instance. The total forces available to repel an invasion on the Norfolk coast were four infantry brigades plus four battalions of cyclists, the equivalent of a Corps of two divisions. Its HQ was at Lynford Manor, near Mundford, a house of 1856-61, now a hotel *[1]*.

1. MUNDFORD, Lynford Hall: HQ of the East Anglian anti-invasion forces in World War I; now a hotel

The regulars of the 12th Lancers had left their barracks in Norwich immediately war broke out, to be followed abroad by many of the regular, territorial, and new battalions of the Norfolk Regiment, along with the Norfolk Yeomanry which went to the Middle East. However the 3rd [Reserve] Bn. Norfolk Regiment spent the War as part of Harwich Garrison, and the 6th [Cyclist] Bn. [TF] spent four years patrolling the Norfolk coast. The battalion was mobilised at North Walsham's Manor Road Board School, the officers' quarters were in the Grange, both officers' and sergeants' messes being in the Kings Arms Hotel. Detachments were based at Thetford, Sidestrand and Worstead at various times.

Also based at North Walsham was an armoured train, four wagons containing machine-guns and two heavier guns, drawn by a locomotive, patrolling East Anglia on the Midland and Great Northern Joint Railway. It had a 12 pounder gun mounted on a converted boiler trolley at each end, then a covered and loop-holed coal truck for infantry, with the 0-6-2 locomotive in the middle. The 14th Bn. Suffolk Regiment [TF], made up of home service men, was based at Weybourne in 1914, then at Sheringham, Holt and finally, by the end of the War, at Cley. It was expected that the coast defences, manned by such units, would delay a landing, the mobile forces would repel it and, failing all else, the field-works of the London Defence Position around the Chelmsford area would halt any further advance on the capital.

In addition, there was an early-warning system of Coastguards and Boy Scouts. At that time the Coastguard was part of the Royal Naval Reserve, so they had all been mobilised leaving a skeleton force in place, many stations having wives holding the fort with Sea Scouts as messengers. Enjoying access to telephones, these coast-watchers provided information about ship movements, mines, and any suspicious events. Provided with radio-receivers, many of these part-time coastguards were able to listen in to German naval traffic, such as that from the Wilhelmshaven naval base, 300 miles [480km] away, thereby providing their controllers at the Admiralty with some notice of intensified German naval activity prior to the Battle of Jutland. [see also Chapter 4] So important did these listening posts become, that the gun-boat, HMS Cricket, mounting AA machine-guns, was permanently stationed off the coast near Hunstanton to protect them from raids by sea or air.

Unlike in World War II when it became increasingly unlikely for there to be an invasion of Britain once Hitler had committed his armies to a Russian adventure, in World War I the threat of invasion failed to recede as the war went on. In fact, it appeared to intensify as a possible way out of the Western Front stalemate for the Germans, and as a way of loosening the naval blockade of Germany. It was therefore deemed necessary to strengthen Britain's fixed defences, particularly in East Anglia. In order to reinforce the existing field-works on the Norfolk coast, a defensive network of pillboxes was planned. The central spine of these defences was a line of circular pillboxes which started on the coast at Stiffkey, ran along past Aylmerton, West Runton and Weybourne, then down the River Ant, past Hanworth, Thorpe Market and Bradfield to North Walsham. Pillboxes survive at all those sites, with several in the North Walsham perimeter and one at Wayford Bridge. In addition there are examples at Bacton and Sea Palling on the Norfolk coast. The basic design is simple. A cylinder of concrete blocks, around 15 feet [4.5m] in diameter externally, has a cast concrete roof. There is a low entrance, closed by a pair of steel doors, and up to

2. MUCKLEBURGH: cylindrical World War I pillbox constructed of concrete blocks, with double steel doors and five loop-holes [TG102434].

five loopholes with hinged steel shutters *[2]*. In some, Aylmerton and Hanworth for instance, these loopholes are at different heights *[3]*. One pillbox at North Walsham is bow-shaped with four loopholes in the curved face, but none in the straight back. According to a recent survey, some twenty of these pillboxes survive in Norfolk, and at least a further dozen have gone. The second pillbox design used in Norfolk was hexagonal and looks very similar to one of the more common designs of World War II. This design is a regular hexagon with sides of around seven feet [2.1m]. One face held a low entrance closed by a pair of steel doors, and there were loopholes in the other five faces. It was built of poured concrete using timber shuttering. The surviving examples include one pair guarding the landward approach to Great Yarmouth *[4]*, along the Norwich road [now the A47], and a singleton at St Olave's boatyard whose office has been built on top.

Anti-invasion defences in World War II

During the inter-War years, little thought was given to coast defence anywhere in Britain let alone in Norfolk. Neither did the period of the Phoney War lend any urgency to the task of defending vulnerable coasts, but the sudden onslaught of the German army with its Blitzkrieg tactics, culminating in the humiliating evacuation of the BEF from Dunkirk in May 1940, forced General Ironside, GOC Home Forces, to plan and implement a realistic defence strategy

3. AYLMERTON: cylindrical World War I pillbox as 2 but the loop-holes have steel shutters and are at differing heights [TG183404].

4. GREAT YARMOUTH: hexagonal World War I pillbox with steel doors and five loop-holes, one of a pair straddling the A47 road [TG506091].

against the invasion which was now anticipated with certainty. The key notion had to be reality. Most of the BEF's armour, vehicles, artillery and even small-arms had been abandoned in France and Belgium. After the necessary rallying and re-organisation, the main factor missing from Britain's only recently-mechanised army, was mobility. Ironside therefore had little option but to build a defensive system based on fixed defences, an unavoidable heresy in the circumstances, but hopefully a time-limited problem, once the munitions factories began to hit higher levels of productivity. Ironside's strategy was to defend the coast as strongly as the available resources allowed, making it as difficult as was possible for enemy forces to land in sufficient strength to form a bridge-head. If the Navy arrived in time from its bases in Rosyth and Scapa Flow to make reinforcement and re-supply impossible, then the initial force could be speedily neutralised. If the enemy were able to move inland however, then successive defensive lines consisting of anti-tank ditches and other obstacles, defended by local troops and the Home Guard with whatever weapons were available, would slow the enemy advance, causing delay rather than attempting a knock-out blow. This would then give the reserves, stationed in Newmarket and Northampton for just such an eventuality, time to move up to the threatened area to defeat the invaders. In the meantime the Navy would have ensured that neither reinforcements nor supplies were allowed to land. The GHQ Reserve which would respond to an invasion of East Anglia included the 2nd Armoured Division in the Northampton area, and the 43rd Infantry Division in Hertfordshire. These formations had identified both locations in which to assemble to tackle particular scenarios, and the code-words which would send them there. The armour would respond to code "George" for instance by grouping in the Thetford/Brandon area, whilst "Percy" would send them into the Fens to meet an invasion from the Wash. The 43rd Division would assemble at Diss to counter an invasion between Great Yarmouth and Aldeburgh, or at Attleborough, in response to a threat from north Norfolk signified by "Nancy".

5. ONGAR HILL: the Battery Observation Post and Right-hand gun-house of the Kings Lynn 6 inch battery which never received overhead cover [TF589241].

The Coastal Crust

As far as Norfolk was concerned, this strategy is very visible. The first layer, called by Ironside the 'Coastal Crust', consisted of several elements. One was batteries of coast artillery, heavy enough to hit landing-barges and their supporting warships at a distance.

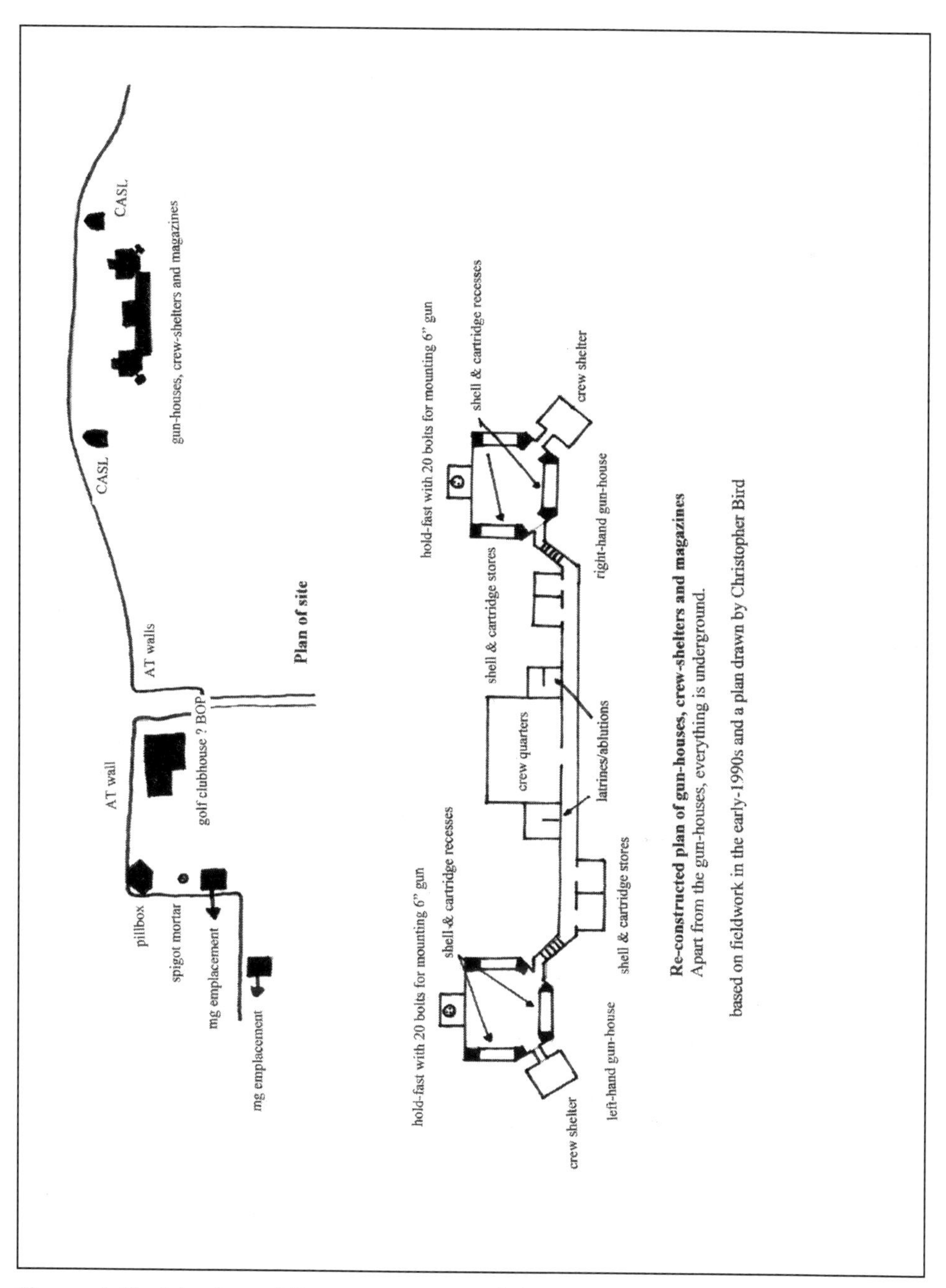

Figure 1 Sketch plan of Brancaster coast defence battery

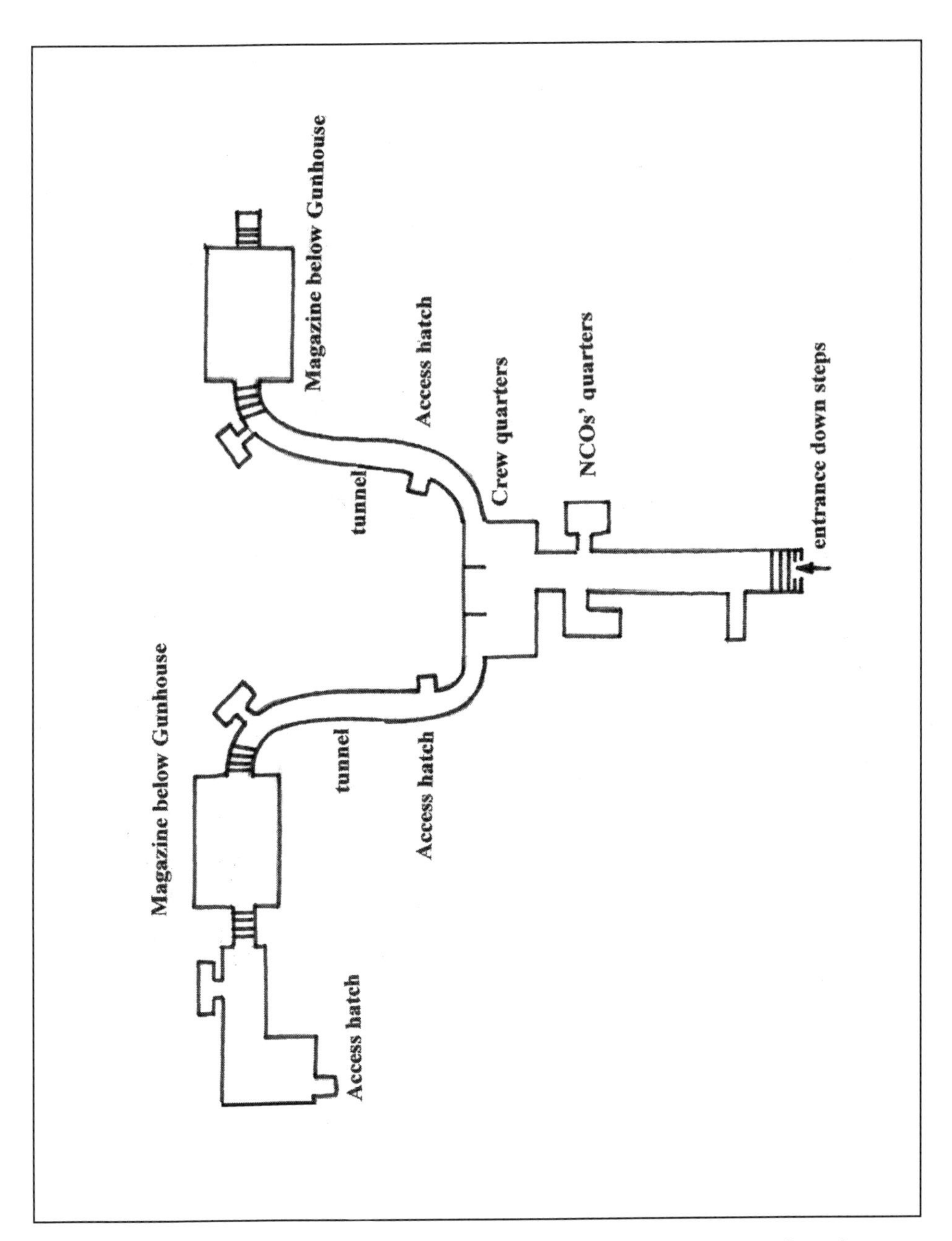

Figure 2 Sketch-plan to show the underground lay-out of Happisburgh coast defence battery

These Emergency Batteries comprised a pair of ex-naval guns, usually 6" but there were some 4.7 inch guns as well, which had been kept in store after their original owners, cruisers of World War I and earlier vintage had been scrapped. An initial list of 46 sites for these batteries was announced in May 1940, and Hunstanton was amongst the very first to become operational by 6 June. Other batteries soon followed at Kings Lynn *[5]*, Cromer, Winterton and Great Yarmouth [North Denes, South Denes, and Links]. The network steadily grew over the next six months with further batteries built at Brancaster *[Figure 1]*, High Cape, Cley Eye, Sheringham, Mundesley *[6]* and Happisburgh *[7]*.

6. MUNDESLEY: the Right-hand gun-house of the 6 inch battery, showing the hold-fast for the gun; the overhead cover has been removed [TG300372].

Each of these batteries had two 6 inch guns apart from Happisburgh *[Figure 2]* with a pair of 4.7 inch guns, and Winterton with two 4 inch guns. These 6 inch guns were of varying age, origin and performance but most fired a shell weighing around 100 lb. [44.5 kg] a distance of about ten miles [16 km]. The Mark 13 had been designed for use in HMS Agincourt one of the class of cruiser, incidentally, in which many local Naval Reserve coast-guards had served in World War I.

7. HAPPISBURGH: the Left-hand gun-house of the 4.7 inch battery [TG375375].

The guns at Cromer had first been installed in the battleship HMS Africa in 1905, and then in HMS Dublin, a cruiser. The smaller 4 inch and 4.7 inch guns fired shells weighing between 30 and 50 lbs [14 and 22 kg], respectively, only a slightly shorter distance. Each gun, with integral shield, either original or made up by a local foundry, was mounted on a hold-fast in a concrete pit, generally provided with a concrete canopy as overhead cover against dive-bombers. Holdfasts may still be seen in several places such as at Mundesley where they have 20 bolts for the 6 inch gun-mountings, and Happisburgh, with 24 bolts for the 4.7 inch guns. The battery at Kings Lynn was abandoned before the overhead cover could be built, so the guns stood open on top of brick and concrete crew-shelters, loop-holed for close defence. Several of the

8. HUNSTANTON: the Coastguard look-out of c1910, which probably served during World War II, as the Battery Observation Post for the 6 inch battery whose magazine lies under the landscaped chapel ruins; there is a small naval type pillbox alongside [TF677421].

Norfolk batteries, including Brancaster, Happisburgh, Mundesley, and Links were of a nucleated design, where the surface gun-houses were serviced by underground magazines and crew-shelters, linked by corridor to each gun-emplacement. Mundesley has lost its overhead cover for the guns. Other batteries such as Kings Lynn, Hunstanton and Winterton, were dispersed with individual components occupying discrete structures within an enclosed area. Visual spotting and instrument range-finding were carried out from a Battery Observation Post [BOP]. At Hunstanton, although the lighthouse had its uppermost floor restored in 1939, the BOP appears to have been on the coastguard tower *[8]*, with a small naval-type pillbox alongside to protect it. Whilst Winterton's BOP was in the lighthouse, Kings Lynn, on a remote site, has a purpose-built three-storey tower. Each battery had two Coast Artillery Searchlights [CASL] in brick and concrete emplacements, usually one on each flank. Generators were housed in solidly-built engine-rooms. An Emergency Battery had a complement of around 150 men who were housed in huts behind the

9. GREAT YARMOUTH, South Denes: bungalows requisitioned as accommodation for the personnel manning Links 6 inch battery [TG530019].

battery. Here also were the workshops, stores, offices and garages. At Links Battery, at the south end of Great Yarmouth, a colony of 1930s seaside bungalows *[9]* was taken over as accommodation for battery personnel. Kings Lynn battery, at the landward end of The Wash, was reckoned to lie too distant from deep water, ever to engage a target worthy of a 6 inch shell, so was closed in 1941, and its precious guns removed to Druridge Bay in Northumberland. The Norfolk batteries were manned by 565th, 546th and 514th Coast Artillery Regiments RA. In common with most Eastern Command coast defence batteries, many of the Norfolk batteries were either stood down in 1943-4, or handed over to the Home Guard. Members of North Walsham's 5 Bn. Norfolk Home Guard were trained to man the Cromer and Mundesley batteries, as were personnel from 11 Bn. at Great Yarmouth for North Denes and Winterton batteries. Both the Sheringham Platoon of 13 Bn. and also elements of Brancaster's manned their local guns. After the war, 514th Regiment was re-constituted, surviving until all coast artillery was stood down in 1956. The emplaced coast artillery guns were augmented by mobile heavy artillery. Keswick Hall was HQ to 57 Heavy Regiment RA, which deployed eight 9.2 inch [23cm], and two 6 inch [15cm] howitzers between Holt, Fleggburgh and Nova Scotia Farm, Caister. As well as these heavier guns, Norfolk's coasts were defended by a number of others. Although Great Yarmouth was not technically a Defended Port, since its fixed defences were part of the Emergency Programme, it was felt that some

10. HEACHAM: gun-house for a 2 pounder AT gun built to drawing number DFW3/28a but with modifications to allow for separate entrances to the two chambers [TF662366].

defence against enemy raids by light craft should be provided. Two 12 pounder QF guns were therefore emplaced on Gorleston Pier, to cover the harbour entrance. There are a number of emplacements for 2 pounder AT guns on the north Norfolk coast at Heacham *[10 & 11]* and at Holme. These are built to the standard War Office design laid out in drawing numbers DFW3/28 and 28a. However, at Weybourne

[12] there is a one-off example which shows no sign of being designed for any particular weapon, so it probably housed a field-gun, possibly a French 75mm, or an 18 pounder. Other field-guns such as old 4.5 inch howitzers, may well have been emplaced in field-works to cover particular beaches.

The Royal Marine 43 Battery was based at Old Catton in Norwich, with eight 12 pounder guns on lorries, ready to respond to emergency calls. As the Home Guard took over the duty of guarding beaches, then some of their sub-artillery weapons were deployed. There are spigot mortar pimples at Holme *[13]*, Walcott, Caister and elsewhere, along with the buildings which housed their bombs. Finally, but long after the threat of invasion had disappeared, the School of AA Artillery at Weybourne installed some 5.25 inch dual-purpose guns in their distinctive emplacements. The War Diaries of II Corps and its constituent formations are full of lists of the wide range of odd guns distributed around the coast. The logistics of supplying ammunition let alone spares to all these units must have been a nightmare and, unsurprisingly, after a while II Corps HQ called a halt to the "manning of fancy equipments eg 6-prs [static] and 4" [static or mobile]" by Field Regiments. The 6 pounders were to go to the GHQ Line and to the Eastern Command Line, the 2 pounders would come out of the beach defences to be used for training, 107 Regiment with its eight 12 pounders would leave the Corps to be re-deployed to London, leaving the remaining RA Field Regiments with mainly 4.5 inch howitzers, and 18 pounder field-guns, ie those guns on which they had been trained, and for which there existed ammunition in quantity. At least one troop of 2 pounder AT guns was retained as part of a mobile column, perhaps one associated with 27 Motor Coach Company RASC, based at Cromer, held in readiness for ferrying reserve troops to trouble-spots.

12. WEYBOURNE: one-off gun-house for possibly an 18 pounder or a 75mm field-gun, with observation post alongside [TG098433].

11. HEACHAM: gun-house for a 2 pounder AT gun built to drawing number DFW3/28a, showing the wide embrasure [TF662366].

13. HOLME NEXT THE SEA: two spigot mortar pedestals on the sea-shore at TF695440; there are two more close by, and a Home Guard store-house a little way inland at TF697440.

Obstacles and obstructions comprised a second element of the Coastal Crust. A minefield extended the length of the east coast in an attempt both to protect the convoys of coastal shipping from naval attack, and to impede the progress of an invasion fleet. Dozens of requisitioned trawlers operated out of Great Yarmouth, patrolling these protected lanes and looking out for enemy mine-laying aircraft. In 1940, the Examination Service, monitoring foreign shipping arrivals was extended to Kings Lynn and Great Yarmouth, with signalling systems, both flags and Aldis lamps, operated initially by Royal Marines, and then by the WRNS. Obsolete World War I torpedo heads, activated electrically by a shore-based observer, were laid in an observation minefield off Great Yarmouth. This was later up-graded into a controlled minefield where mines could be selectively exploded under specific targets, having been illuminated by Ryder searchlights. Cromer Pier was seen as a potential landing-stage for enemy raids so, having had it requisitioned under the provisions of the Defence of the Realm legislation, the local RE unit blew holes in it. Minefields out to sea were complemented by mined beaches. A five-mile-long [8km] boom stretched across the Wash, made of nets suspended from canvas tubes, whose buoyancy was aided by kapok. On 11 May 1940, the order went out from II Corps HQ for the immediate fortification of Great Yarmouth, Lowestoft and Weybourne with wire and trenches.

This was only the beginning, and eventually, pretty well the entire Norfolk coastline was obstructed with scaffolding hung with anti-personnel mines and barbed wire; with steel stakes embedded in concrete just below the high-water line, designed to tear the bottoms out of landing-barges; and large anti-tank blocks, usually five foot [1.2m] cubes, often on concrete rafts for added stability in the shifting sands. One idea, born of desperation, was the flame-barrage which consisted of a pipeline through which fuel could be pumped onto the beach, and then ignited in the face of enemy landings. It is possible that the pipeline below Stiffkey Camp *[14]* may represent such an attempt. Beach exits were blocked by more rows of

AT blocks, and road-blocks formed from slotted concrete blocks and RSJs.

A little way inland, routes from the coast were blocked by vertical steel rails inserted into concrete sockets, or by hairpins, or by portable concrete AT cylinders, which could be rolled down slopes into the path of vehicles. Examples of some of these measures can be seen behind the beaches on the coast near Castle Rising *[15]* and Heacham, for instance. Flame-fougasses, adaptations of devices used since the seventeenth-century, would spew burning oil onto vehicles attempting to move inland off the beaches. Many bridges or defiles on

14. STIFFKEY: it has been suggested that this pipeline across the marshes was originally built to convey petrol as part of a flame barrage; it is overlooked by a circular World War I pillbox [TF967440]. A more likely explanation is a sewer-pipe.

routes leaving the immediate beach area were set up as demolitions that could be triggered in the event of an invasion, once the defending forces had fallen back behind them. Road-blocks had to be designed so as not to impede legitimate traffic up to the last moment, but to be capable of speedy closure, a matter of fine timing. On non-essential routes, they could be staggered, with two semi-closures 40 yards apart, and coils of wire, and other obstacles, placed ready to effect closure. Mindful of problems with prematurely-obstructed main routes in France during the retreat to Dunkirk, major roads could only be narrowed to 20 feet [6m], and staggered road-blocks were forbidden. Village defences were to incorporate road-blocks, but disassembled, with the materials piled beside the road for

15. CASTLE RISING: sockets for AT rails on a bridge over the Babingley River, here acting as an AT ditch [TF673256].

use at the appropriate time. This problem of mobility also prompted a number of other measures. The REs of 18 Division, with their HQ in the Cattle-market drill hall in Norwich, were required to construct and maintain emergency pontoon-bridging equipment at St Olaves, in case the bridge there was destroyed by either side, and access was needed for a counter-attack.

A third element of the Coastal Crust defences was the strings of pillboxes built along the cliffs and dunes of the Norfolk coast, replacing many of the field-works initially constructed. The sheer multiplicity of designs testifies both to the piecemeal rather than systematic approach, and the speed and urgency with which the task was undertaken. A suite of official designs was issued by the Directorate of Fortifications and Works at the War Office in May 1940. Some of these were bullet-proof with walls 12-24 inches [30-61 cm] in thickness, whilst others were shell-proof with walls 25-54 inches [62-137 cm] thick. The official instruction stated that those constructed on beach-exits should be shell-proof, whilst all others could be bullet-proof. Both types should have reserve positions to fall back to. They include square, hexagonal and rectangular designs, and examples of most of these may be seen on the Norfolk coast. However, one may also see odd examples of designs found elsewhere in greater numbers, or single examples of one-off local designs not found anywhere-else. The grand plan was set down by Eastern Command but, at a local level, group contractors worked with RE officers to fill in the pieces of the jig-saw, construction being carried out by local builders. The design of the structure which subsequently appeared on the ground was influenced by local conditions, availability of materials, tactical considerations, and personal preference. Contractors were urged to economise on materials, particularly cement, and it was inevitable that compromises were made, often reducing the effectiveness of the defences. However, vulnerable landing places such as Weybourne, for instance, were quite strongly fortified. Along the shoreline and the cliff-top, are a line of machine-gun posts, sited to enfilade the beach. A little way behind these on high ground, are other clusters of machine-gun posts firing directly out to sea, supported by an emplacement for a field-gun, with its own OP. Farther back, is a line of pillboxes, designed to stop any infantry who might have slipped through the forward cordon, and, behind these, is yet another line of machine-gun posts covering exit points from the beach area. All that, of course, represents only what is visible sixty years on. What we can only see from contemporary

16. WEYBOURNE: hexagonal shell-proof pillbox given a range of loop-holes enabling a variety of automatic weapons to enfilade the beach [TG097440].

plans, are all the obstacles and field-works which complemented the more substantial elements of these defensive arrangements. William Foot took Weybourne as one of his

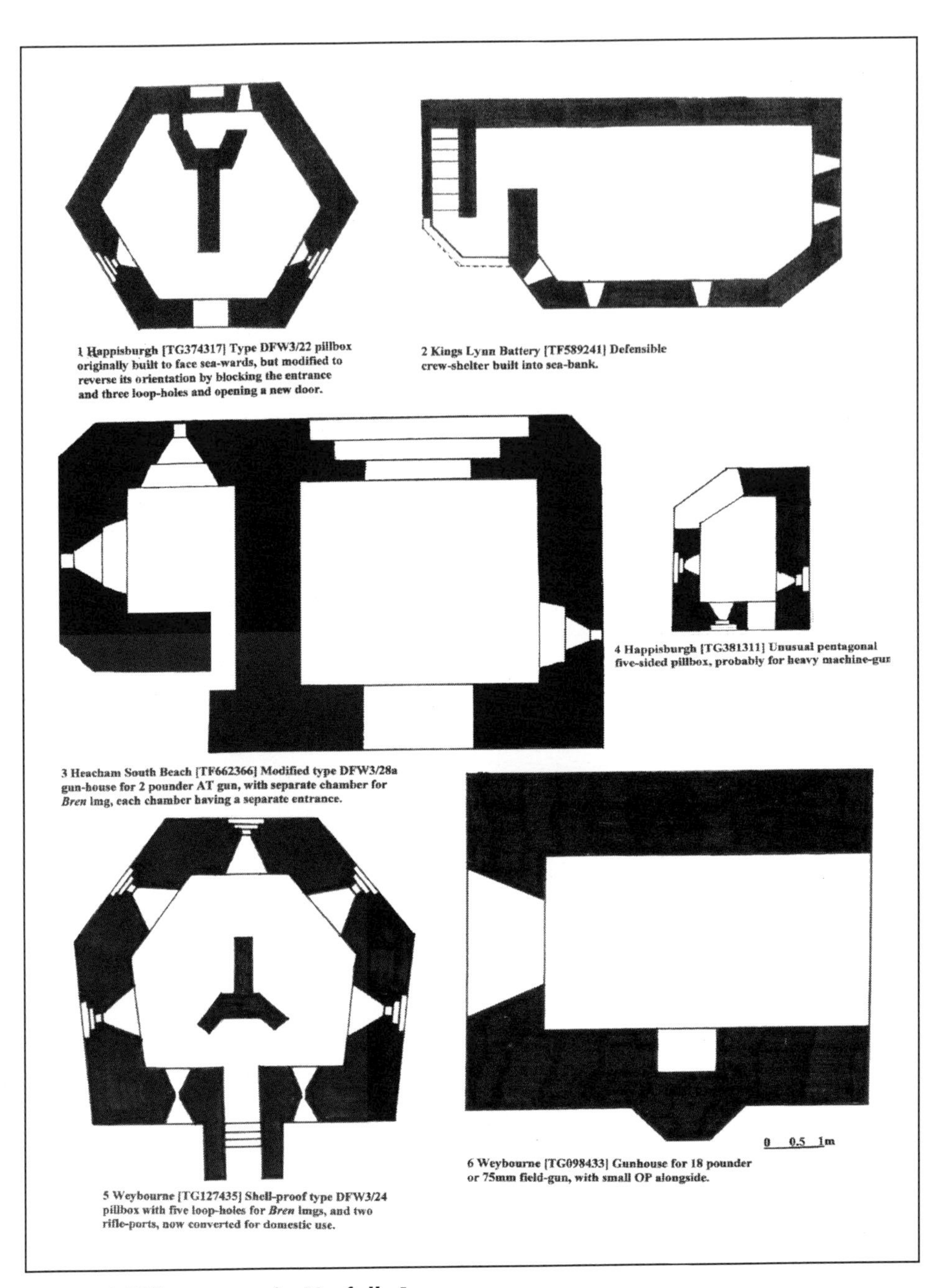

Figure 3 Pillbox types in Norfolk 1

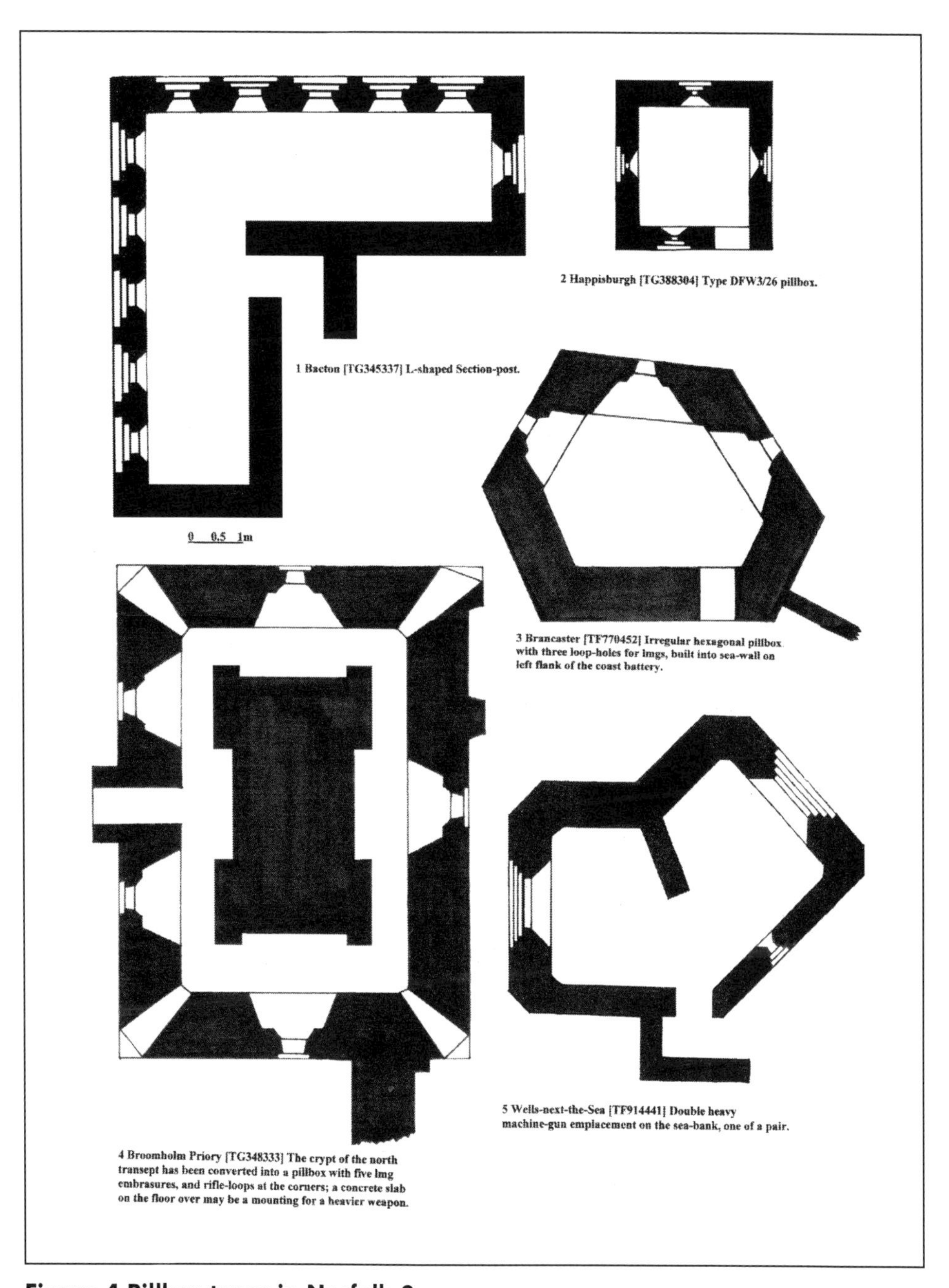

1 Bacton [TG345337] L-shaped Section-post.

2 Happisburgh [TG388304] Type DFW3/26 pillbox.

3 Brancaster [TF770452] Irregular hexagonal pillbox with three loop-holes for lmgs, built into sea-wall on left flank of the coast battery.

4 Broomholm Priory [TG348333] The crypt of the north transept has been converted into a pillbox with five lmg embrasures, and rifle-loops at the corners; a concrete slab on the floor over may be a mounting for a heavier weapon.

5 Wells-next-the-Sea [TF914441] Double heavy machine-gun emplacement on the sea-bank, one of a pair.

Figure 4 Pillbox types in Norfolk 2

1 Weybourne [TG097438] Shell-proof machine-gun post, one of a range of non-standard designs loosely-based on a War Office plan of 1936.

2 Weybourne [TG097440] Shell-proof hexagonal pillbox with loop-holes for lmgs and rifles, sited to enfilade the beach.

3 Hellesdon, Norwich [TG201112] Shell-proof hexagonal pillbox built as part of the City's defensive perimeter. [after Peter Kent]

4 West Raynham [TF858246] Circular pillbox with loop-holes at two levels, and tunnel entrance. [after Peter Kent]

5 Ludham [TG402189] Shell-proof pillbox built for airfield defence [after Peter Kent].

6 Coltishall [TG275229] Shell-proof pillbox with five monopod mounts, built for airfield defence [after Peter Kent]..

Figure 5 Pillbox types in Norfolk 3

17. GIMINGHAM: hexagonal pillbox to drawing number DFW3/22 with a roof parapet and a Hazzard mount for a 20mm Oerlikon LAA gun [TG295377].

18. HAPPISBURGH: square pillbox to drawing number DFW3/26 [TG388304].

case studies, and lists 32 pillboxes of six different known designs, emplacements for AT guns, field-guns and seven more for machine-guns, OPs and an Allan Williams turret. Then there are mine-fields, barbed-wire and scaffolding obstacles, lengths of AT ditch, slit-trenches and rifle-pits, an emplacement for a beach-light, and spigot mortar pits. In total, there are ninety-odd separate installations along a 2.5 mile [4 km] stretch of coastline. These were manned by a territorial battalion and a further battalion of the Home Guard, plus detachments of gunners, engineers and signallers from the parent 53 Brigade of 18th Infantry Division, a second line TA division which included men of the Cambridgeshire, Norfolk and Suffolk Regiments. The 4th Bn. Norfolks were at Great Yarmouth, the 2nd Bn. Cambridgeshires at Stiffkey, whilst the 5th Bn. Suffolk Regiment covered the sector containing Horning, Acle, Mundesley and Stalham. The other major formation operating across the Norfolk/Suffolk border at this time, was the 55th Infantry Division whose HQ was near Diss. As the war went on, many of these units were removed to be posted overseas. When a battalion of the South Staffordshire Regiment left the Burnham Market-Kings Lynn sector in 1942, they left a void for the Home Guard to fill. Tragically, 18 Division was sent to Singapore just in time for the surrender to the Japanese.

A wide variety of designs for pillboxes *[Figures 3-5]* was used on the north Norfolk

19. WEYBOURNE: one of a number of similar shell-proof emplacements for Vickers machine-guns based on the War Office design of 1936 [TG097438].

coast. The suite of drawings issued by the War Office Directorate of Fortifications and Works Department 3 [DFW3] included those

20. BACTON: L-shaped section post with eleven loop-holes [TG349337].

for AT guns noted at Heacham and elsewhere [DFW3/ 28 and 28a] plus bullet-proof and regular shell-proof hexagonal pillboxes [DFW3/ 22 & 24] *[16 & 17]*, square bullet-proof pillboxes [DFW3/ 26]*[18]* and a basic shell-proof Vickers machine-gun emplacement *[19]*. In addition

21. BRANCASTER: irregular hexagonal pillbox with three loop-holes for lmgs, part of a strong-point on the left flank of the coast-defence battery [TF770452]

to these designs, there were L-shaped section-posts which can be seen at Bacton *[20]* and Cromer; irregular hexagonal pillboxes *[21]*, and a whole range of machine-gun emplacements derived from the DFW3 model, including a double

22. HOLKHAM: double machine-gun pillbox one of a pair defending the coastal railway-line, here marking the rear-most defence line behind the beach defences; there are several pairs of these structures in this area [TF879442]

version at Holkham *[22]*, Cley and elsewhere, but not outside Norfolk. Another type of such variants can be seen at Weybourne *[23&24]*.At Happisburgh is an odd five-sided pillbox with a large embrasure *[25]*. The Allan Williams turret is a small, domed revolving steel turret mounting lmgs in both ground and LAA modes *[26]*. They are found all over Britain in small numbers, but appear to have been particularly popular in Norfolk, being used in coast defence at Cley Eye and Salthouse, for instance. Wartime photographs show

23. WEYBOURNE: a 'before' picture of a one-off pillbox built to enfilade the beach from the cliff-top; it has two compartments for different weapons.

one on top of a building at the landward end of Cromer Pier. Many of these pillboxes were camouflaged, one of the least-easily seen, being built into a tower of Broomholm Priory *[27&28]*. At least two half- pillboxes were built onto the ends of buildings, outside Great Yarmouth at White House Farm, and at Postwick overlooking the River Yare. Some permanent posts were built less solidly. In the back-garden of a house at Ingham Corner, Lessingham in what was

24. WEYBOURNE: the 'after' picture showing conversion into a bird observatory [TG127436]; close by is a shell-proof hexagonal pillbox built to drawing number DFW3/24, now converted as accommodation [TG127435].

25. HAPPISBURGH: one-off pentagonal pillbox probably designed for a heavy machine-gun [TG381311].

26. HOLKHAM: a well-preserved Allan Williams turret; its revolving cupola contained lmgs in both ground and LAA roles [TF894439].

27. BACTON, Broomholm Priory: the crypt of the North Transept of this 13th Century Cluniac foundation has been converted into a block-house with five lmg embrasures, as seen here in the blocked doorway, and a widely-splayed rifle-loop in each corner [TG348333].

28. BACTON, Broomholm Priory: one of the lmg loops; also shown is the texture of the corrugated-iron sheets used as shuttering for the poured concrete.

probably the rear line of the coast defences, is a concrete platform with iron fittings. This formerly had sand-bagged walls and a corrugated-iron roof supported on corner-posts. It was for a 0.303 inch [8.5mm] Vickers machine-gun manned 24 hours a

29. INGHAM OLD HALL: loop-holes in the boundary wall of this manor-house, probably used as a local HQ [TG393261].

day by the local Home Guard. There was another at neighbouring Moor Road, Sutton, overlooking Sutton Broad and the Stalham boat-yards. Between the two is Ingham Old Hall, with a loop-holed wall *[29]*. Lyon beach-lights were apparently in short supply, and there seem to be none of their characteristic emplacements to be seen on the coast of East Anglia. Given the shortage of both materials and labour, existing structures were often adapted as defence works. A number of drainage mills, Ludham *[30]* and Stracey Arms, for example, had loop-holes cut into the walls, and fighting platforms inserted where necessary. Barns such as one at Halvergate for instance, could be loop-holed in order to command a particular road-junction or area of open ground. Sometimes an entire building was turned into a strongpoint. The World War I Repair Shed at RNAS Great Yarmouth was a good example. This was a rectangular, brick-built structure lying parallel to the sea-shore on the eastern edge of the old airfield. In the 1940 adaptation, one end was strengthened with concrete walls, in which were inserted four rifle loops. At the other end, two chambers were formed, one containing two machine-gun embrasures with fixed mountings, and the other having six rifle-loops, three in each face. Just up the road at the Naval Hospital, dual-purpose loop-holed air-raid shelters were built against the perimeter walls. Many more such conversions and adaptations must have existed which have either been demolished or bricked up and plastered over.

The Y Service in Norfolk in World War II

A vital part in the intelligence-gathering process was the Y Service, for listening in to

30. LUDHAM BRIDGE: drainage mill adapted as a strong-point by the addition of loop-holes and firing-platforms; a spigot mortar pedestal stands alongside [TG372172].

enemy radio transmissions. As in World War I, posts were set up all over Britain, with one on the Norfolk coast at Winterton, and others at Trimingham, opened in May 1941, and at Beeston, Sheringham. Information from these was sent directly to Bletchley Park, often, presumably only in the case of the non-urgent, by motor-cycle courier. These posts were run by the Admiralty, and the RAF ran a separate, but similar, operation at Gorleston, aimed at picking up signals from mine-laying ships and aircraft, sending the information through a filter-room at Harwich, hoping to be able to intercept these intruders by sea or air.

Inland defence lines

The second plank in Ironside's defence planning consisted of continuous, linear AT obstacles, supported by concrete fixed defences- pillboxes and gun-emplacements, known generically as Stop Lines *[Figure 6]*. At a national level, the GHQ Line, extending from the Bristol Channel to the Medway, and from thence across the Thames and north to the Welland, ultimately reaching the River Tay, provided a shield, behind which, reserves might be gathered, in order that they might be deployed against an invading force which had punctured the coastal crust and its back-up defences. At Command level, corresponding linear defences were constructed to further delay the enemy's advance. One arm of the Eastern Command Line originated in Colchester, and ran up the rivers Colne, Stour and Lark, via Wakes Colne, Sudbury, Bury-St Edmunds and Mildenhall. The other arm, sprang from the Ipswich defences, and followed the rivers Gipping, Black Bourn and Little Ouse via Stowmarket, Thetford and Brandon. They come together either side of Littleport on the Great Ouse, and run from thence to Kings Lynn on the Wash, with a spur running from Downham Market along drains past March to the Nene at Guyhirn. At the next level,

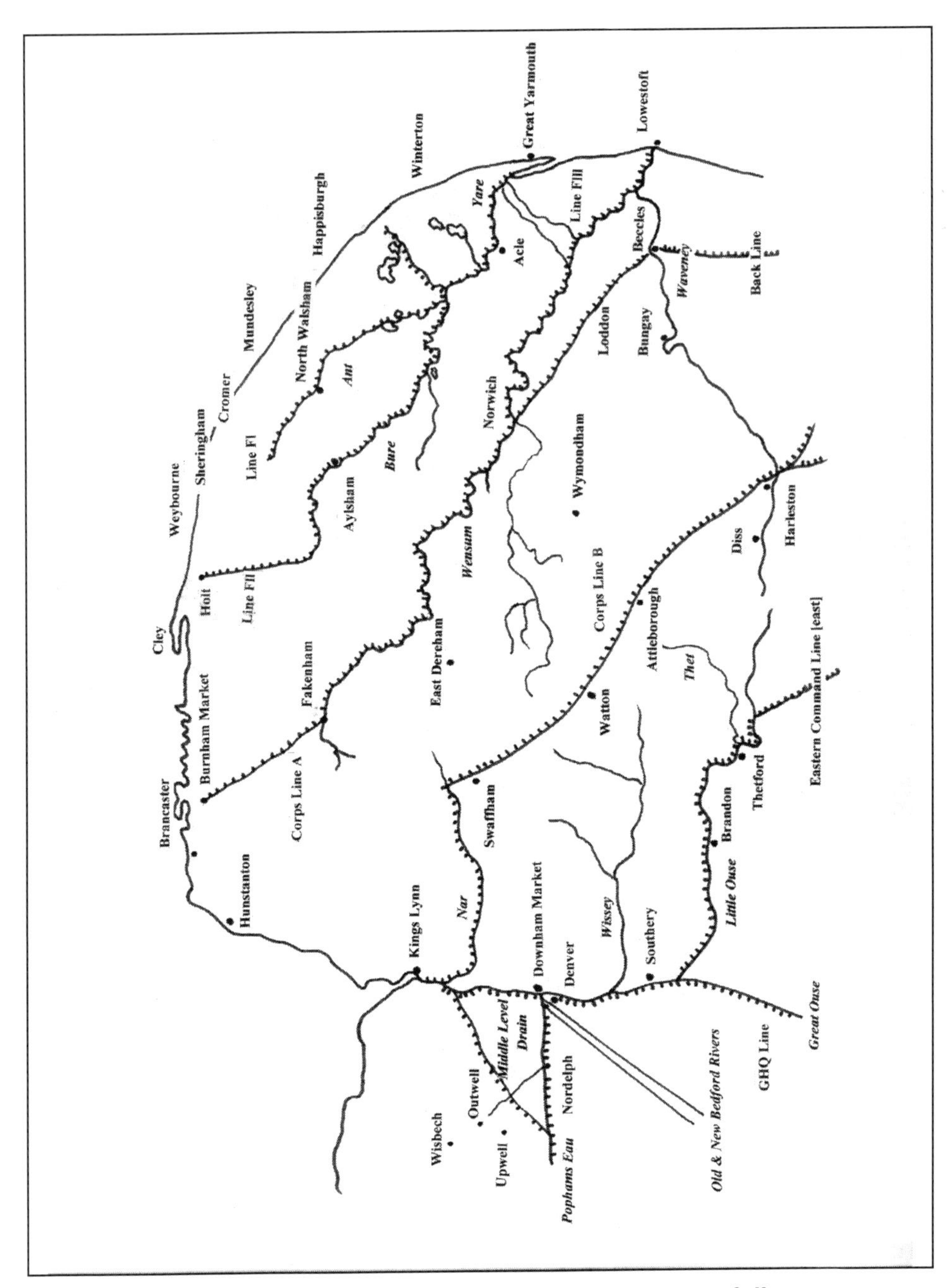

Figure 6 Map to show Defence Lines and Nodal Points in Norfolk

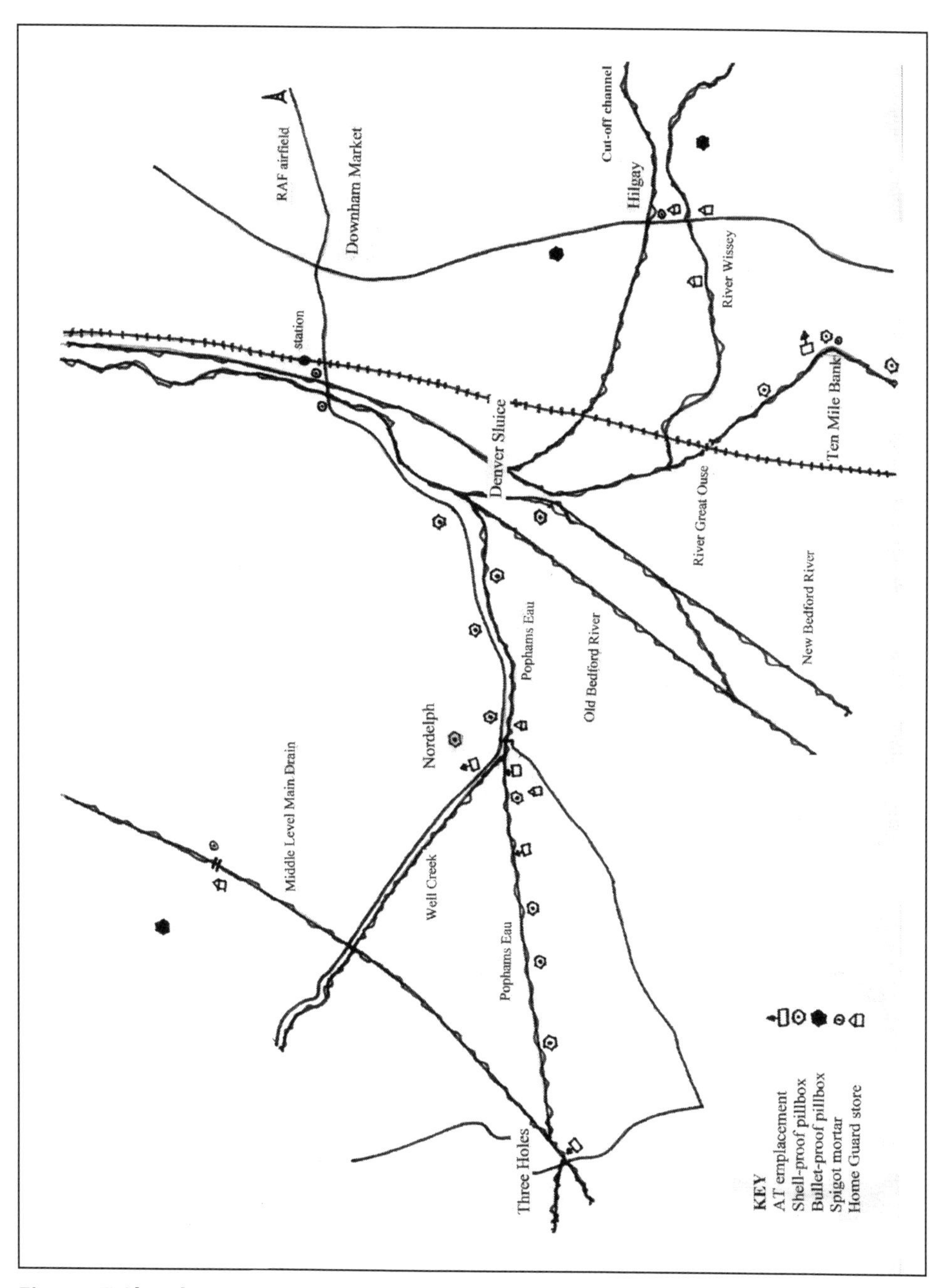

Figure 7 Sketch map to show Defence Lines in west Norfolk

there were four Corps Lines in Norfolk. Line FI ran from North Walsham to the coast near Horsey, along the rivers Ant and Thurne, its southern stretch, echoing the defence line of World War I. Line FII began near Holt, picking up the River Bure, north of Saxthorpe, which it then followed to Great Yarmouth via Aylsham, Wroxham and Acle. Line A ran from Burnham Market through Fakenham, along the river Wensum to Norwich where it split into two, the main line continuing through Loddon to Beccles, and Line FIII running along the river Yare through Reedham to Lowestoft. These three F lines appear on the military maps of the time primarily as demolition belts, where bridges over waterways would be mined. Finally, Line B began at Kings Lynn and ran via Swaffham, Watton and Attleborough to Harleston, where it forked, with the northern arm meeting the coast at the mouth of the river Blyth at Walberswick, and the southern arm somewhere near Thorpeness. In addition to these defence lines, there was a hierarchy of defended towns. The most important were designated as Defended Places, capable of being held independently by their local garrisons, Norwich and Kings Lynn coming into this category. Other towns which occupied strategic locations on roads, railways or rivers, often junctions or bridging points, were labelled Nodal Points, and fortified accordingly. Many of Norfolk's nodal points were located on the lines described above, but the additional designated nodal points of Diss, East Dereham and Wymondham occupied important locations in the region's communications network. It is worth noting that were an invading force sufficiently unfortunate as to select a landing beach around, say, Sea Palling, they would have had to have negotiated no less than twelve stop lines prior to rolling into Trafalgar Square.

The Eastern Command Line in Norfolk

The stronger, western arm of this line which started in Colchester, and ran through Bury-St-Edmunds and up the river Lark only entered Norfolk after it had already run a few miles down the River Great Ouse to reach Southery. By then, it had joined with

31. POPHAMS EAU: hexagonal shell-proof pillbox to drawing number DFW3/24 on this extension of the Eastern Command Line [TF537008].

the north-western end of the eastern branch of the line which enters Norfolk just below Thetford, following the River Little Ouse to Brandon Creek. Although both Thetford and Brandon were defended as nodal points [dealt with in Chapter 2], out in the intervening countryside the main strength of the line lay in the river acting as an AT ditch without very much extra reinforcement. There are a number of spigot mortar positions, notably at Santon Downham and on the outskirts of Thetford itself. These are of the local pattern with a hexagonal thimble which, owing to the high water-table, is set within a concrete retaining wall instead of the more normal sunken pit. West of Brandon, a couple of pillboxes and some AT blocks occur where the line was considered most vulnerable. Once the Great Ouse has been reached, then the defences are stronger with concentrations of AT emplacements and pillboxes at Brandon Creek and Ten Mile Bank. The village of Hilgay, on the river Wissey in advance of the main line is defended by a pillbox and a spigot mortar. The existence of two separate Home Guard explosives and inflammables stores would suggest that there were originally more defences here. The river crossings at Downham Market are defended by spigot mortars, as are some of the crossings on the Middle Level Drain which converges on the Great Ouse below Kings Lynn. There are also remains of defences along the river Old Nene, making a third line of defence along the Norfolk border. The heaviest defences, however, are along the spur which follows Pophams Eau to the river Nene beyond March *[Figure 7]*. In the six miles [9.5 km] between Denver Sluice and Three Holes, there are still 12 shell-proof pillboxes, four AT emplacements, two Home Guard stores, several spigot mortar thimbles, and AT blocks and rails. Most of the pillboxes are built to designs originated by the DFW3, in drawings numbered 22, 24, 28 and 28a. The first is a small hexagonal bullet-proof pillbox with loopholes in five faces, and a door with or without a loophole in the sixth face. The DFW3/ 24 is a shell-proof irregular hexagon designed for five lmgs, with a door flanked by two rifle-loops in the longer rear wall *[31]*. The DFW3/ 28 is a gun-house for either a 2 pounder AT gun, or a 6 pounder Hotchkiss QF gun, and the DFW3/28a is the same but with a lmg compartment to one side *[32]*. The version for 2 pounder AT gun has a wider embrasure, recesses for the gun's split trail in the front wall, and a socket in the floor for the gun's pivot. The version for the Hotchkiss gun has a narrower embrasure, with a pedestal carrying a hold-fast with nine fixing bolts for the gun to be

32. POPHAMS EAU: gun-house for 2 pounder AT gun with integral chamber for Bren lmg built to drawing number DFW3/28a [TF546009].

mounted. It is doubtful whether any guns were ever mounted as these were prepared positions rather than permanently manned ones, and guns were in short supply. Initially, the Hotchkiss guns had come without mounts, which had to be improvised by each individual unit, until II Corps came up with a standardised fitting.

33. ACLE: small brick pillbox built on to end of Manor House facing down the village street [TG403105].

Norfolk's other defence lines

Line F1 can be traced along the river Ant from Bradfield Bridge above North Walsham. Many of the pillboxes are re-used ones from World War I, but they are supported by machine-gun emplacements and both bullet-proof and shell-proof pillboxes. At the lower end of this line there is a particularly strong position at Ludham Mill where the River Ant is crossed by the main road from Wroxham. Here the old drainage mill has been converted into a strongpoint by the addition of loopholes and firing-platforms. Alongside is a spigot

34. HALVERGATE: loop-holed barn commanding approach to a road junction [TG418073].

mortar position, and there are also a pillbox and a Home Guard store. A similar concentration of defences may be seen at Wayford Bridge, where the Norwich road to Stalham crosses the River Ant. Here, along with a World War I pillbox, are a machine-gun emplacement, a pillbox, and two spigot mortars. More pillboxes are found at Dilham and Honing, with AT rails protecting the former rail-crossing at Briggate Mill.

Line FII appears to have its origin in Letheringsett, a little east of Holt, where a cluster of spigot mortars with a Home Guard store guard a crossing of the River Glaven. The nodal point of Aylsham is defended by at least three pillboxes, and there are pillboxes and AT blocks scattered along the River Bure at Brampton, Buxton, Horstead and Wroxham. The area of the Broads, between Wroxham and Acle seems not to have needed fixed defences, relying on the water itself and the River Patrol. Acle is a nodal point with pillboxes at Fishley, a disguised pillbox attached to the manor-house *[33]*, more pillboxes to the south of

35. POCKTHORPE: AT blocks guarding a crossing on Corps Line A, the River Wensum Line [TG072178].

the town, and a spigot mortar guarding Wey Bridge. South of the river, Tunstall and Halvergate *[34]* are defended, and the Stracey Arms mill, an ideal observation point, was loop-holed. Towards the east, the river joins the Great Yarmouth defences.

Line A starts at Burnham Market which is surrounded by pillboxes. To the south-east at Egmere lies a defended cross-roads with three shell-proof pillboxes, two spigot mortars and a Home Guard store. South of Fakenham, a nodal point, the line joins the River Wensum which it follows to Norwich. The northern and eastern defences of Swanton Morley airfield properly belong to this line, and there are others, mainly AT Blocks and the odd Home Guard store-house, at Pockthorpe *[35]*, Lenwade and Ringland. Covering the bridges at Mill Street, east of Swanton Morley, at least one spigot mortar emplacement survives. Placed on a low river-bank, prone to flooding, the thimble is contained within a low wall at ground level, rather than down in a pit, a relatively rare arrangement but one seen elsewhere in East Anglia. Norwich, as a defended place, sits astride the line which re-emerges on the east side of the city, and then splits in two. The main line drops down along the line of the Beccles road [now A146 and B1140] with defences, mainly pillboxes and spigot mortars, evident at Ashby St Mary, Thurston, Hellington, Loddon, and Raveningham. The other line, FIII, follows the River Yare as far as Reedham, then the railway line to Haddiscoe and Somerleyton *[36]*, and on

36. SOMERLEYTON: AT blocks forming part of a complex rail-block on the railway bridge over the River Waveney where the Great Yarmouth-Beccles line formerly crossed over both the river and the Lowestoft-Norwich line [TM451986].

37. HADDISCOE: hexagonal pillbox next to the high-level signal-box and platform of the railway station [TM460985].

along the railway and the River Waveney together, to Oulton Broad where it enters the western perimeter of the Lowestoft defences. Haddiscoe *[37]* is strongly fortified, both round the road bridge, with pillboxes, loop-holed wall and spigot mortar, and also at the point at which the old railway from Great Yarmouth to Beccles crossed the River Waveney, protected by rows of massive AT blocks, AT rails and a spigot mortar.

Line B's most likely course from Kings Lynn is along the River Nar to Castle Acre, then due south along the road to Swaffham. Many of the river-crossings such as High Bridge, Blackborough, that near Abbey Farm, in the centre of Narborough and above Narford Hall are all defended with AT rails *[38]* of different types, pillboxes and spigot mortars. From Swaffham to Watton, both nodal points, the line most probably followed the former railway, much of which is either on embankments or in cuttings, creating a continuous and effective AT obstacle. Two pillboxes still stand on the outskirts of Swaffham where roads ran under the railway, and another remains by the railway-bridge south of Holme Hale. From Watton to Attleborough, and on to Harleston, there appears no obvious route for Line B. A string of six pillboxes, at roughly three mile intervals, between Thetford and Harleston, probably indicates a line of 1940 search-light sites. There are a few clues east

38. NARBOROUGH: bed of 36 'hairpin' AT rails on the north side of the River Nar [TF764144].

of Attleborough- a block-house built onto a house at Besborough, and loop-holes in the churchyard wall at Pulham Market, then a clear railway-line/stream to Harleston, which was defended as a nodal point. The line then crosses into Suffolk, heading for Halesworth where it splits, with one arm heading east for Blythburgh and Walberswick, and the other dropping south by the railway line to Saxmundham, forming part of the Back Line [Beccles to Manningtree].

Armoured trains

As in the previous war, East Anglia was found to be particularly suitable for the operation of armoured trains which offered another way of providing mobility. A total of twelve trains were assembled, six for use in Scotland, and six for East Anglia. Each train consisted of two modified steel coal wagons, one at each end, mounting a 6 pdr. QF Hotchkiss gun, a Vickers heavy machine-gun, a Boys AT rifle, and twin Bren lmgs on an AA mounting. The truck was armoured by pouring four inches [100mm] of concrete between the two steel skins, and sheet-steel shields were added for extra protection at head-height. Two modified drop-side wagons carried supplies, and a Class F4 ex-Great Eastern 2-4-2 locomotive was coupled in the middle of the train. In July 1940, Train 'G' was based at Melton Constable, and carried out patrols along the lines between Kings Lynn and Great Yarmouth, with branches to Wells, North Walsham and Cromer. The programme was never extended as planned, so some trains, originally assigned to East Anglia, had to be redeployed to other Commands. Train 'A' had originally been based in Norwich but was one of those given up to another Command, moving to the St Albans / Bletchley area, and also, for a while, to Devon. Train 'G' was moved to its new base at Heacham, later widening its patrol area to include Thetford. Firing practice was carried out by shooting into the Wash from the Heacham area. As the regular army units moved away to overseas duties, then the contribution of the armoured trains in supporting the Home Guard became more significant. Many of the armoured train units developed their reconnaissance role by acquiring light armoured vehicles. Train 'G' had three armoured 30cwt Bedford trucks at Heacham in 1942. These were armoured with steel plate, and loop-holed for use by AT rifles and light automatic weapons. The War Office also made available four Bren-gun carriers, to give the unit a wider repertoire. From 1941, many of the trains had been crewed by Polish troops, but the passive nature of the patrolling, and the diminishing threat of invasion, proved a frustration to these lively troops. One particular railway problem was the provision of AA cover for freight trains, and it was found that loading a light tank, mounting a quadruple 7.92mm Besa machine-gun, onto a ramp-wagon provided one solution. This idea, which was to prove highly successful, was tested out in Norfolk. By late 1943, all the armoured trains had been de-commissioned, Train 'G's final patrol, to Fakenham and Wells, having taken place in April.

The Auxiliary Units

The likelihood of invasion was taken so seriously in the summer of 1940, that plans were put in place to establish a secret, underground guerrilla force. The task of this force would be to harass the invaders by using terrorist methods to tie up troops in guarding lines of communication, and by disrupting the supply chain. Nominally part of 202 Bn. Home Guard,and often referred to as the British Resistance Organisation, these men operated in small units of around half-a-dozen, being trained to use weapons and explosives, and in a range of clandestine warfare techniques such as concealment, sabotage, intelligence-gathering and unarmed combat. They operated out of Operational Bases [OBs] which were cunningly concealed in preferably remote spots, usually underground. A standard OB was a buried Nissen hut with brick end-walls, entered through a hatch, and with an escape tunnel at the far end. Each OB had bunks, food and water, weapons, ammunition and explosives. The majority of OBs were in the countryside, but there were three in Norwich, for instance, on Earlham golf course, now UEA, on Plumstead Road and Marston Lane. Norwich personnel met up, incognito of course, and ignorant of each other's status and activities, at the Veterans' Club in Princes Street. Another OB was in the basement of a tower at Baconsthorpe Castle. Each cell operated separately, not knowing where neighbouring cells were, or who was in them. The whole operation was secret, and auxiliaries tried to pass themselves off as normal Home Guards, particularly to family and friends. Membership was by invitation, and recruiters tended to go for poachers and game-keepers and others who knew the land and were happy living off it. At its peak there were 201 Auxiliaries in Norfolk, operating in 35 units with 40 OBs and eight more planned. The HQ was at Beeston Hall near Neatishead, with a control and communications centre at Rackheath Hall outside Norwich. Training took place on Cawston Common, and at Leicester Square Farm, Syderstone. In the last few months a site has surfaced in Waveney Forest which may well be connected to the Auxiliary Units. In an area of the Somerleyton Estate, known to have contained several OBs, a complex of eight underground storage cells has been found, each the size of a freight container, with a thick concrete roof supported by iron stanchions and shuttered in corrugated-iron. Some of the walls have been tanked with tar or pitch, and some then covered in Hessian and chicken-wire. Entry was through a hatch in the roof, about 18 inches [45cm] square, and there was also, adjacent to this, a small ventilation hole in each. Whilst these storage facilities are fairly near to the Admiralty sidings, they are remote enough for it to be unlikely that they were connected. It is quite possible that caches of weapons and explosives were established here for the several patrols operating in the area. It is to be hoped that further investigation will reveal their function, although, as yet, local enquiries have uncovered few clues. Only in the mid-1950s, were former auxiliaries allowed to talk about their activities, but many still preferred to keep mum, only opening up in their old age. Their national museum is in the watch office at Parham airfield near Framlingham [Suffolk] where artefacts and documentation may be seen.

Other anti-invasion measures

As well as the trawlers patrolling the shipping lanes and looking out for enemy mine-laying activity, the Auxiliary Patrol Service, mainly in armed trawlers, were on the watch for any signs of invasion, acting as an early-warning system. Similar activities were undertaken on inland waterways by the Broads Patrol, under the auspices of the Royal Navy, but seen as part of the Home Guard. This consisted of 26 boats based at Wroxham, with moorings at Acle, Brundall, Ormesby, Potter Heigham and St Olaves. They were manned by their pre-War skippers and crews, each boat being fitted with a Lewis gun, mounted on a post, amidships. Often dismissed at the time as "wooden, rich men's afternoon-tea boats", and as sitting ducks to aircraft attack, they were probably useful in the remoter Broads for watching out for parachutists, and, of course, like many Home Guard efforts, good for morale. A similar force operated at Kings Lynn, where a Home Guard river patrol of motor-boats had its HQ at the Ouse Sailing Club.

As well as obstructing beaches against sea-borne landings, it was also necessary to prevent the use of flat, open spaces for airborne landings by gliders or parachutists.

To this end, many such areas were planted with scaffolding-poles and wires, or old farm carts or even automobiles with their wheels removed, filled with earth or rubble. Old Buckenham Common, for instance, was planted with vertical telegraph-poles, in staggered lines. In some places, a chequerboard of trenches was dug to obstruct gliders.

The Norfolk Broads were seen as particularly inviting to enemy float-planes and were defended accordingly. Breydon Water, for instance, was provided with a 75mm field-gun, [later substituted for an 18 pounder gun] to be mounted in an emplacement with 15 inch thick [38cm] walls, and with nine Vickers 0.300 [7.62mm] machine-guns, later reduced to four. These were to be mounted in Cowan emplacements built of concrete blocks. Where either there was a lower risk or the weapons just were not available, expanses of water were simply obstructed, and appropriate obstacles were suggested by HQ 18 Division. These included rafts of oil-drums wired together, and branches of trees, tied together and anchored to the lake-bed. It was also suggested that, wherever it could possibly be contrived, vertical spikes should be mounted. Motor cruisers were moored across Hickling Broad as an obstacle against float-planes, an operation which, as Christopher Bird recently pointed out, preserved them for further generations of boating holiday-makers.

One of the most important lessons on the World War I Home Front, had been the value of co-ordinated information, in order to gauge a particular danger, and the appropriate levels of response. Nationally accepted code-words such as Cromwell, were used to define the state of perceived threat, but these had to be understood and disseminated in a controlled way. Norwich adopted a system whereby information relating to an invasion was reported to the military at Britannia Barracks, to the RAF at Horsham St Faith, to the Air Ministry at Stoke Holy Cross radar station, and to the Police Staff Officer at HQ. Local code-words such as Seagull to denote various levels of threat were also adopted. A deluge of undifferentiated information over inadequate 'phone lines was recognised as a potential problem, so a number of telephone battles were organised by II Corps, in August 1940, to test the performance of signallers and staff officers down to battalion level, and also including Corps reconnaissance troops, and the liaison channels with Bomber Command at RAF Wyton [Cambridgeshire]. It is, of course, totally logical, but nevertheless deeply ironic, that both the effectiveness and the efficiency of the anti-invasion measures increased as the likelihood of an invasion diminished.

THE DEFENCE OF VULNERABLE POINTS 2

During World War I there may never have been a belief in the absolute certainty of invasion, but many on the Home Front, particularly those in the direct path of an invading army across the North Sea, nevertheless felt insecure. Partly as a result of this unease, and partly owing to the prevailing desire of people, even those forced to stay at home, to do their bit for the defence of their country, many volunteered for quasi-military duty. In December 1914, the inaugural meeting of the Volunteer Training Corps [VTC] was held at the Assembly Rooms in Norwich's Agricultural Hall. This organisation, similar to the Home Guard of the next war, was intended to mobilise those in reserved occupations or otherwise exempt from military service, both to release troops for more important duties, and to engage those at home psychologically with the war. By Christmas, 600 had enrolled and were attending drills on Earlham Road Recreation Ground. There were similar initiatives elsewhere, Hunstanton's Lounge Pavilion hosting a VTC recruitment meeting on 21 May 1915. Volunteers were organised into patrols which guarded stretches of railway line, and key locations such as Scowle swing-bridge. Particularly sensitive locations such as the listening-posts in Hunstanton, were provided with sentries. Uniforms were worn, and old soldiers trained volunteers to shoot, ranges being constructed specifically for their use such as that at Wortham Ling near Diss. However unfairly though, there was always a feeling that the VTC provided a refuge for those who sought to avoid proper military service. The public perception though, was of superannuated volunteers, their GR armbands suggesting words like "Grandads" and "relics". As well as the VTC, there was the Civilians' Emergency Corps which raised 1200 members in Norwich. Their task was to manage the operation of civilian transport, either offered voluntarily as a result of public appeals, or requisitioned by local Emergency Committees. In the event of invasion, this fleet would be used for transporting troops, supplies or casualties as necessary. Whilst understandably ambivalent about the status of volunteers, the army generally appreciated the efforts made by civilians to ease the constant manpower shortages. Public hysteria, never far from the surface, could at least be diverted into constructive and reassuring activity this way.

Vulnerable points in World War II

If the previous war had offered only the slight possibility of invasion across the sea, then this time there was a much greater likelihood of invasion, and a greater variety of ways in which it might happen. The development of new technology, on both sides, meant that not only was vulnerability deemed to have increased, but greater also was the variety of assets to be protected. Apart from the invasion coast itself, Norfolk was home to port facilities essential to the success of an invading force, to large numbers of important operational airfields, to several links in the radar chain which warned of impending aerial attack, to camps and training grounds where new armies were to be grown, and to the web of transport systems which sustained the production and distribution of essential food-stuffs and munitions. The enemy now had the means to destroy or merely to disrupt this infrastructure through raids by air or sea. There was a real fear, after the experiences in Belgium and Holland, that parachutists would descend in large numbers to secure airfields for incoming transport aircraft carrying armoured vehicles and artillery. Waterways might afford sea-borne troops ways through the defences enabling them to strike at the country's heartlands. Leaving out the obvious route across the Straits of Dover, attacks could, from mid-1940 onwards, be mounted from anywhere on the coastline from Belgium to Norway, from western France, or from Ireland. More worryingly, all these routes were within the range of bombers with fighter cover. It was imperative that everything was guarded all the time.

Airfield defence in World War II

Airfields by their very nature are vulnerable to attack from land, sea, and, especially, from the air. Any defence scheme had to take into account several eventualities. One was the possibility of a direct assault on the airfield itself by airborne troops. Another was an attack by troops landed elsewhere by air or by sea. A third involved being over-run in the course of a general invasion, and a fourth envisaged the involvement of fifth columnists supporting clandestine attack. In summer 1940, Major-General Taylor, Inspector General of Fortifications at the War Office was tasked with assessing the relative risks, and of formulating measures to address them within the resources of the time and material available. He decided that location should be the key criterion for deciding the level at which fixed defences should be provided. Hence all airfields within twenty miles [32km] of a designated sea-port, would be deemed Class 1, qualifying for the highest level of defence provision. In Norfolk, Kings Lynn and Great Yarmouth were classed as sea-ports which might become targets in the course of an enemy invasion, so any airfield within the agreed radius was to be given this level of fixed defences. This was set at 20-32 pillboxes, some facing inwards to repel an enemy air-landing, and others facing outwards, to defend against external assault. Provision was also made for dummy pillboxes to draw enemy fire and mislead enemy dive-bombers. The majority of Class 1 airfields were also provided with Pickett-Hamilton Forts, the so-called "disappearing pillboxes". Given the shortage of man-power, an attempt was also made to determine the optimum manning level for the garrison of an airfield. For Class 1

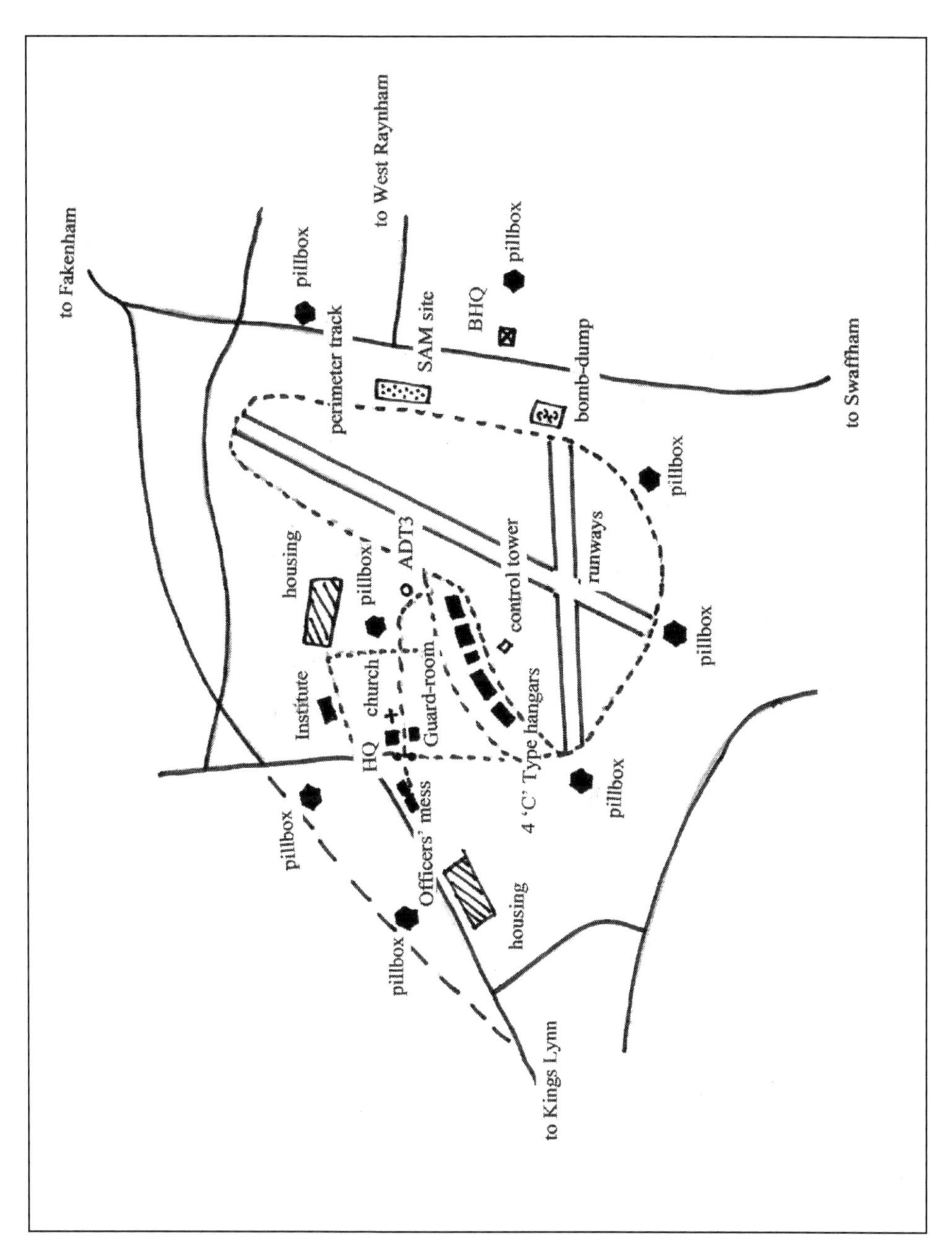

Figure 8 Sketch plan of West Raynham airfield showing salient features and defences

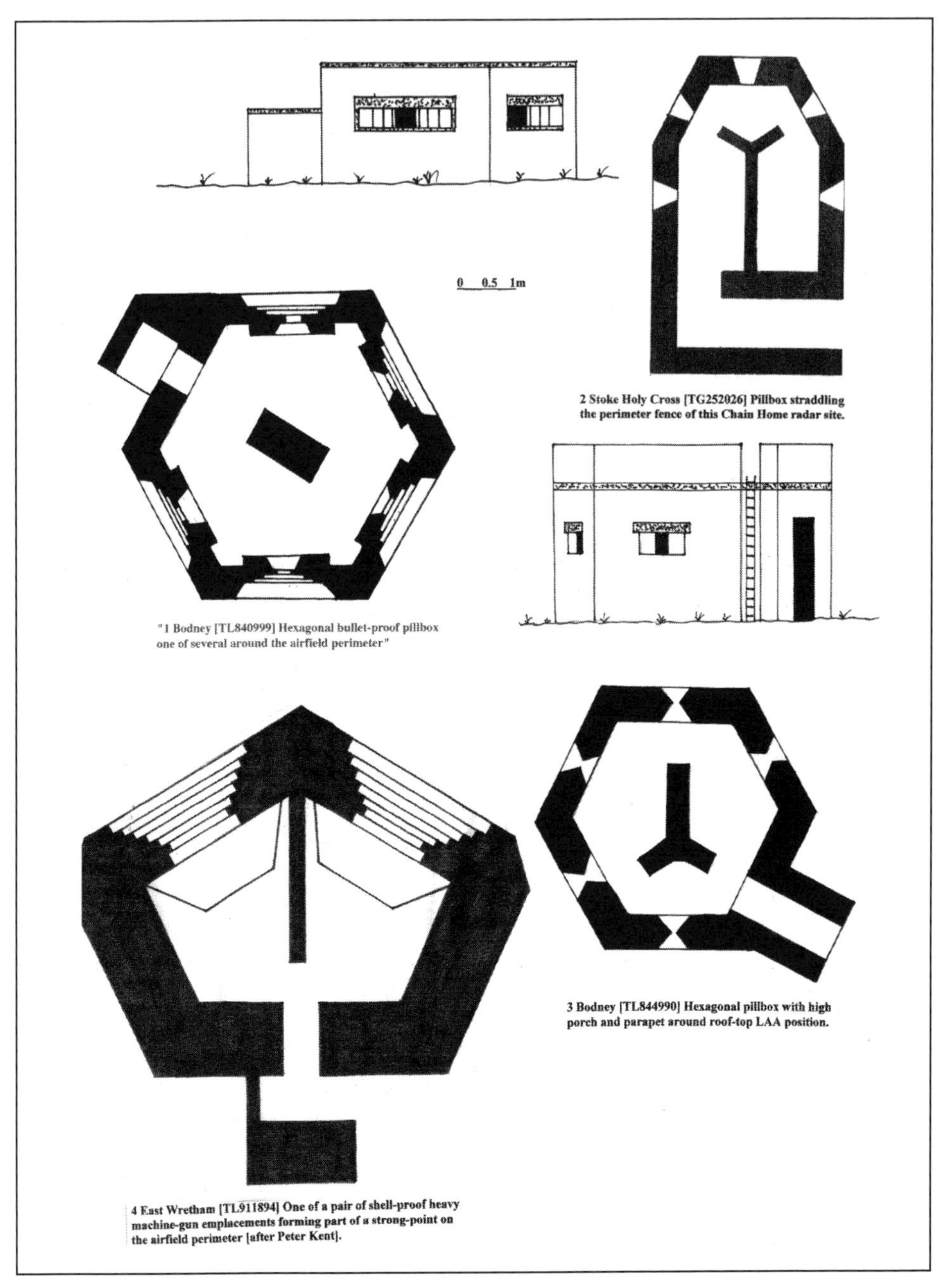

"1 Bodney [TL840999] Hexagonal bullet-proof pillbox one of several around the airfield perimeter"

2 Stoke Holy Cross [TG252026] Pillbox straddling the perimeter fence of this Chain Home radar site.

3 Bodney [TL844990] Hexagonal pillbox with high porch and parapet around roof-top LAA position.

4 East Wretham [TL911894] One of a pair of shell-proof heavy machine-gun emplacements forming part of a strong-point on the airfield perimeter [after Peter Kent].

Figure 9 Pillbox types in Norfolk 4

39. FELTWELL; Airfield Battle HQ [11008/41] commanding the flying area and looking over to the hangars of the Expansion Period, and the radomes of the Cold War [TL703887].

40. BARTON BENDISH: fairly standard hexagonal bullet-proof pillbox to drawing number DFW3/22, its brick shuttering beginning to peel off revealing the concrete core [TF718047].

airfields, this was set at 274 men. This was only the army contingent, drawn in Norfolk from, amongst others, the 1st Bn. Cambridgeshire Regiment. It was expected that the RAF would organise defence platoons from their ground staff and any other available personnel, under the command of supernumerary or under-employed RAF officers. Rudimentary armoured vehicles were extemporised from trucks and civilian cars, in order to provide some element of mobility in the defence, however basic. The defence was co-ordinated from a Battle HQ *[39]*, in the early days a converted building or adapted pillbox, but from 1941, a standardised purpose-built structure, built to Air Ministry drawing number 11008/41. Also in 1941, the RAF Regiment was formed, primarily for airfield defence. This released troops back to the army, but would also have to compete for the same recruits. The defence of airfields against air attack [see Chapter 4] was usually the responsibility of AA Command, but AA guns were normally integrated into the general defence, with gunners being taught how to engage ground targets. Since, in the early days at least, no AT guns were issued, the 3.7 inch HAA gun was the only available weapon effective against armour. It was also common for RAF and, later on USAAF personnel, especially on bomber- stations, to put some aircraft machine-guns or cannon on improvised mountings in an AA role. Some of these were mounted on trucks or jeeps, turning them into versatile additions to the ground defence's armoury as well. Whilst the initial defence layout tended to be linear *[Figure 8]*, with two concentric rings of pillboxes circling the airfield's perimeter, as tactical ideas developed, there was a move toward the establishment of strong-points with all-round defence, distributed around key points of the airfield, an analogue to the nodal point approach at the macro level.

41. BODNEY: one of several hexagonal bullet-proof pillboxes built to a slightly larger specification than the standard DFW3/22 [TL840999].

Possibly owing to the urgency involved in carrying out the construction of airfield defences in Norfolk, many of the pillboxes are either based on the simplest DFW3/ 22 design, or are local non-standard models *[Figure 9]*. Examples of the former may be seen at Bircham Newton, Barton Bendish *[40]*, Docking, Marham and Coltishall, and of the latter, at Ludham and Coltishall. Adaptations of DFW3/ 22 designs may be seen at Matlaske where a shell-proof, thickened version stands, at Bodney, where there are four slightly larger than standard examples *[41]* and one with a roof LAA position *[42]*, and at West Raynham, where half-a-dozen examples remain of a small version which would fit inside the standard model. At Feltwell and Methwold *[43]* are examples of standard DFW3/ 26s, square

42. BODNEY: one-off hexagonal pillbox with projecting full-height porch, and roof parapet with LAA mounting [TL844990].

pillboxes with four loopholes and a low door. There are, however some quite elaborate local one-off designs. A couple of circular pillboxes with tunnel entrances and loopholes at two levels survive at West Raynham *[44]* but nowhere else, and there are two different horseshoe-shaped mg emplacements at Oulton Street. Also at Oulton Street *[45]* and at Horsham St Faith's are examples adapted from an octagonal design favoured more in Scotland. As with the other contexts in which pillboxes were employed, they were part of a complex system of trenches and weapons pits, wire and other obstacles, and mines.

The disappearing pillboxes, or Pickett-Hamilton forts were allocated to most Class 1 airfields, and this included 15 in Norfolk, thirteen of which formed the major part of the second priority group nationally. Interestingly, the list included both Norwich and Horsham St Faith, which would suggest that someone in the War Office or Air Ministry was unfamiliar with the local geography. The Pickett-Hamilton fort comprised a concrete loop-holed cylinder which sat inside a slightly larger cylinder set in the ground. When in the down position the roof was at ground level. Action stations saw the crew of two sprint across the grass,

43. METHWOLD: square pillbox, one of a pair built to drawing number DFW3/26 [TL737945].

go in through a hatch in the roof, and raise the fort by means of pneumatic pressure from a compressed air bottle, or manually if that system failed. In a raised position, the trio of forts installed at the junctions of

44. WEST RAYNHAM: unusual circular pillbox, one of two with tunnel entrance and loop-holes at two levels, found only on this airfield [TF859247].

45. OULTON STREET: octagonal pillbox with solid semi-circular machine-gun table set at one of its seven loop-holes, and two AR walls [TG151278].

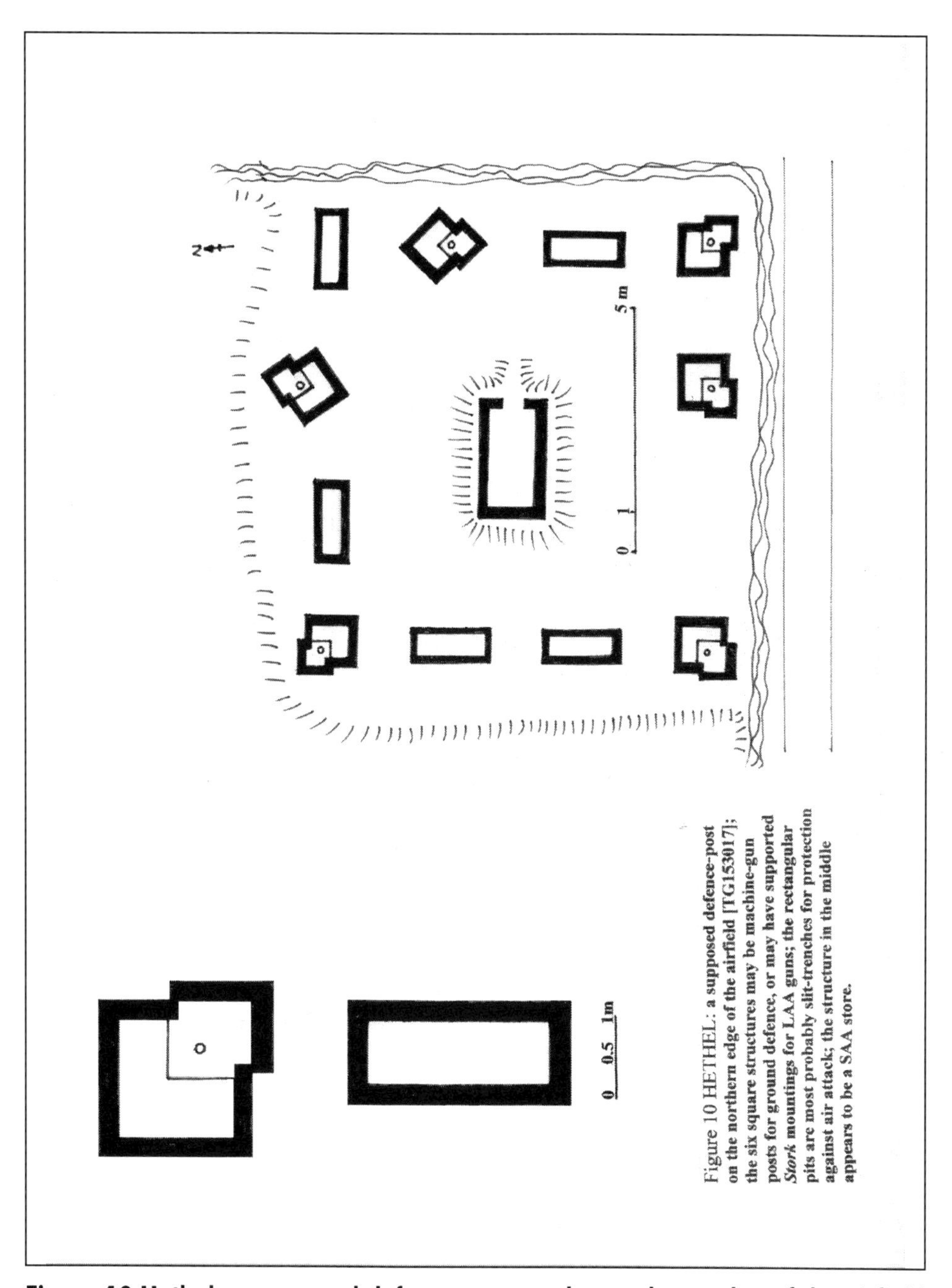

Figure 10 Hethel: a supposed defence-post on the northern edge of the airfield

46. EAST WRETHAM: double machine-gun emplacement with two chambers, each having a table for a Vickers gun; one of a pair, which along with two pillboxes and a SAA store, formed a defended locality in the airfield defences [TL911894].

runways, could command the landing-area with automatic fire. The key concept was that when friendly aircraft landed the forts were sunken, and when the enemy were trying to land, they were raised. Although they impressed Churchill greatly, they were unreliable, ineffective and dangerous to the users. Although 335 were constructed by the New Kent Company of Ashford, Kent and installed on 124 airfields, they were considered neither reliable nor even particularly useful.

There are a number of examples in Norfolk of the standard Air Ministry drawing number 11008/41 Battle HQ design. This consists of several sunken rooms for PBX, messengers etc, with a concrete-roofed cupola with 360 degree observation slit, which enabled the garrison commander to co-ordinate the defence of the airfield with benefit of all-round visibility over the flying field. It is entered through a hatch next to the cupola, with another entrance at the other end down stairs to the messengers' room. Examples of these may be seen at Bodney, Feltwell, West Raynham, Langham, and Methwold, with a slightly different one at Thorpe Abbotts. Others of this pattern existed, but have been demolished, as at Wendling and Hardwick, for instance. Also demolished, but to a different design, Air Ministry drawing number 11747/41, were the Battle HQs at Docking and Horsham St Faith. Yet another example of a local design, since demolished, stood at Coltishall, at the eastern end of the hangar arc.

It is possible to see evidence of the policy of grouping structures into self-defensible pockets at a number of Norfolk airfields. At East Wretham, there is a strongpoint composed of two twin machine-gun emplacements *[46]*, two hexagonal bullet-proof pillboxes, and an ammunition store, in a square area which would have been surrounded by wire, with trenches linking the five major structures, all commanding one corner of the airfield. This was replicated on the other side of the airfield. At Bodney, the BHQ and adjacent pillbox may represent a strongpoint, developed out of the otherwise conventional pattern of a ring of seven pillboxes around the airfield perimeter. A unique arrangement on Hethel's northern boundary may be another *[Figure 10]*. Here, a square enclosure, bounded on two sides by a boundary-ditch, contains what appear to be five brick-lined slit trenches, six square brick-lined pits with sides of six foot [1.8m], and raised plinths, three foot six [1.07m] square, in outward-facing corners, and a central, semi-sunken store-house. Set in the plinths are monopod mounts, and they present themselves as either machine-gun emplacements or bases for LAA Stork mountings. This may have been one of several such complexes since destroyed by agriculture or later uses of the airfield by Lotus cars.

Attempts to inject mobility into airfield defence started with the Armadillo, a generic term for armoured trucks. A wooden box structure with loop-holed hollow walls filled with shingle was bolted onto the truck's flat bed, creating a compartment for two or three men with rifles and a Lewis gun, but lacking overhead cover. They replaced the wholly impracticable Bison, which was basically a concrete pillbox on wheels. Small family saloons like the Standard 14 hp. were fitted with steel sheets over oak planks to produce a rudimentary armoured vehicle. These, the first such models to be produced in quantity,

47. WEST BECKHAM: hexagonal bullet-proof pillbox built to drawing number DFW3/22 [TG141390].

were named Beaverettes after Lord Beaverbrook, then Minister of Aircraft Production, who first commissioned them. Given that the evidence on the ground would suggest that nowhere were pillboxes built in the numbers which the Taylor Report seemed to require, it is possible that the numbers were made up by use of these mobile defence posts, often in conjunction with field-works. Official airfield plans seldom record fixed defences, but usually include open blast shelters which may have been regarded as defensible, and the boomerang-shaped slit trenches which were also dual-purpose.

48. STOKE HOLY CROSS: one of a pair of hexagonal pillboxes whose design is unique to this site; this one, straddling the boundary dacoit fence, has a Hazzard mount for an Oerlikon 20mm LAA gun on its roof [TG253025].

Many of the pillboxes built to defend Norfolk's airfields have survived. There must be Pickett-Hamilton forts still buried beneath airfields, as at Horsham St Faith, but one visible survivor at Thorpe Abbotts, now an aviation museum, in fact was removed from Martlesham Heath [Suffolk].

The defences of Radar sites

Radar sites were so important to Britain's defences, that they were protected not only against the general threat of invasion, but, more particularly against enemy raiding parties who might land with the express purpose of capturing top-secret equipment for analysis back in Germany. Ironically, the success of the British raid on the German radar site at Bruneval, on the Normandy coast in 1942, may have served to increase the perceived risk of such a retaliatory operation. Some radar sites such as Bard Hill [CHL], Happisburgh [CHL], Hopton [CHL], Winterton [10cm] and Trimingham [10cm] were located directly on the invasion coast and so were protected in the general scheme of things, usually with pillboxes, DFW3/ 22s at Happisburgh and Trimingham, machine-gun emplacements and spigot mortars at Bard Hill. West Beckham [CH] and Stoke Holy Cross [CH] were a little way inland, consequently being provided with stand-alone defences. At West Beckham there are DFW3/ 22 pillboxes *[47]* around the site, and DFW3/ 26 ones on top of the Receiver and Transmitter Blocks. At Stoke Holy Cross there are standard DFW3/ 22s outside the site, but straddling the fence around the heart of the site, are two pillboxes unique to this location *[48]*. They are hexagonal with five loopholes facing to the outside, and one has an inward-facing loophole as well. One carries a Hazzard mount for a 20mm Oerlikon LAA gun. All these radar sites were constantly guarded by either regulars or the Home Guard. The 5th

49. THORPE ST ANDREW, Norwich defences: AT block sited to constrict traffic under a railway bridge [TG273085].

50. COSTESSEY, Norwich defences: two of the three remaining AT blocks on a disused railway track; one is reinforced with a length of rail [TG195103].

Bn. Norfolk Home Guard based on North Walsham, for instance, was given the responsibility for mounting guards at the Happisburgh and Trimingham sites, as well as RAF Mundesley [sic], which may have been a detached site for personnel manning the radars. Other, similarly sensitive VPs included the RN W/T station at Ormesby.

Norwich and Kings Lynn: Defended Places

The city of Norwich sat astride Corps Line A, but was designated a Defended Place, capable of all-round defence with its own garrison. Within 48 hours of the setting up of the Local Defence Volunteers, over 1800 men had enrolled in Norwich. Its defence was based on a simple defended perimeter, initially consisting of a ring of 16 pillboxes, and gradually being strengthened by AT obstacles, manned road-blocks covered by weapons pits, and Dannert wire barriers. There are still places where these defences remain. There are AT blocks and rails and a sunken pillbox at Hellesdon, AT blocks along the line of the railway at Thorpe St Andrew, another pillbox and a spigot mortar at Catton, and a spigot mortar in Earlham Park overlooking the bridge over the River Yare. It would appear that the perimeter ran

51. KINGS LYNN: some of the group of twenty or so remaining AT rail sockets outside the East Gate on Broad Walk [TF625197].

52. EAST DEREHAM: pillbox guarding level-crossing, now restored by the RBL as a memorial [TF994131].

from the railway at Thorpe St Andrew in the east, around the River Yare on the south and south-west, up the River Wensum on the west, and through the line of RAF Horsham St Faith and Sprowston in the north. Railway lines or rivers provided continuous AT obstacles for around two thirds of this 20 mile [32km] circuit, but AT ditches were necessary to complete the defences, as for example across Catton Park as far as Spixworth Road. The main routes out would have been sealed by road-blocks of hairpins, bent rails fixed into sockets in the road. Even a track which runs underneath the railway near the cemetery east of Thorpe Bridge *[49]*, is constricted by a large AT block, and a rail-block of three large AT blocks, two of them 5' [1.5m] cubes, and the third reinforced by lengths of railway-line, straddles the now-deserted railway at New Costessey *[50]*. The core of Norwich's garrison was the City's three Home Guard battalions, the 6th, 10th and 16th Bns. Norfolk Home Guard, each assigned a sector of the city and its surroundings. Training often took place on Mousehold Heath, an area of wilderness used, in previous wars for training by the cavalry. There were a number of vulnerable points in the city, some of which such as the Unthank Road telephone exchange were guarded every night. There was a dedicated railway Home Guard company formed from around 80 or so LNER employees, and these had the specific task of guarding the Railway Control Room, the Thorpe Junction signal box, and Thorpe Station itself. Their twin explosives and inflammables stores may still be seen behind the station. As well as the Home Guard, the Norfolk Regiment's Infantry Training Centre [ITC] based in Britannia Barracks provided reserves to be deployed as necessary. These included a mobile column comprising the HQ

53. THETFORD: gun-house for a 2 pounder AT gun converted to an infantry pillbox behind the 'Ark' PH; the embrasure for the gun, whose split trail would have fitted into the slots visible at ground level, has been blocked to form two loops for Bren lmgs [TL876834].

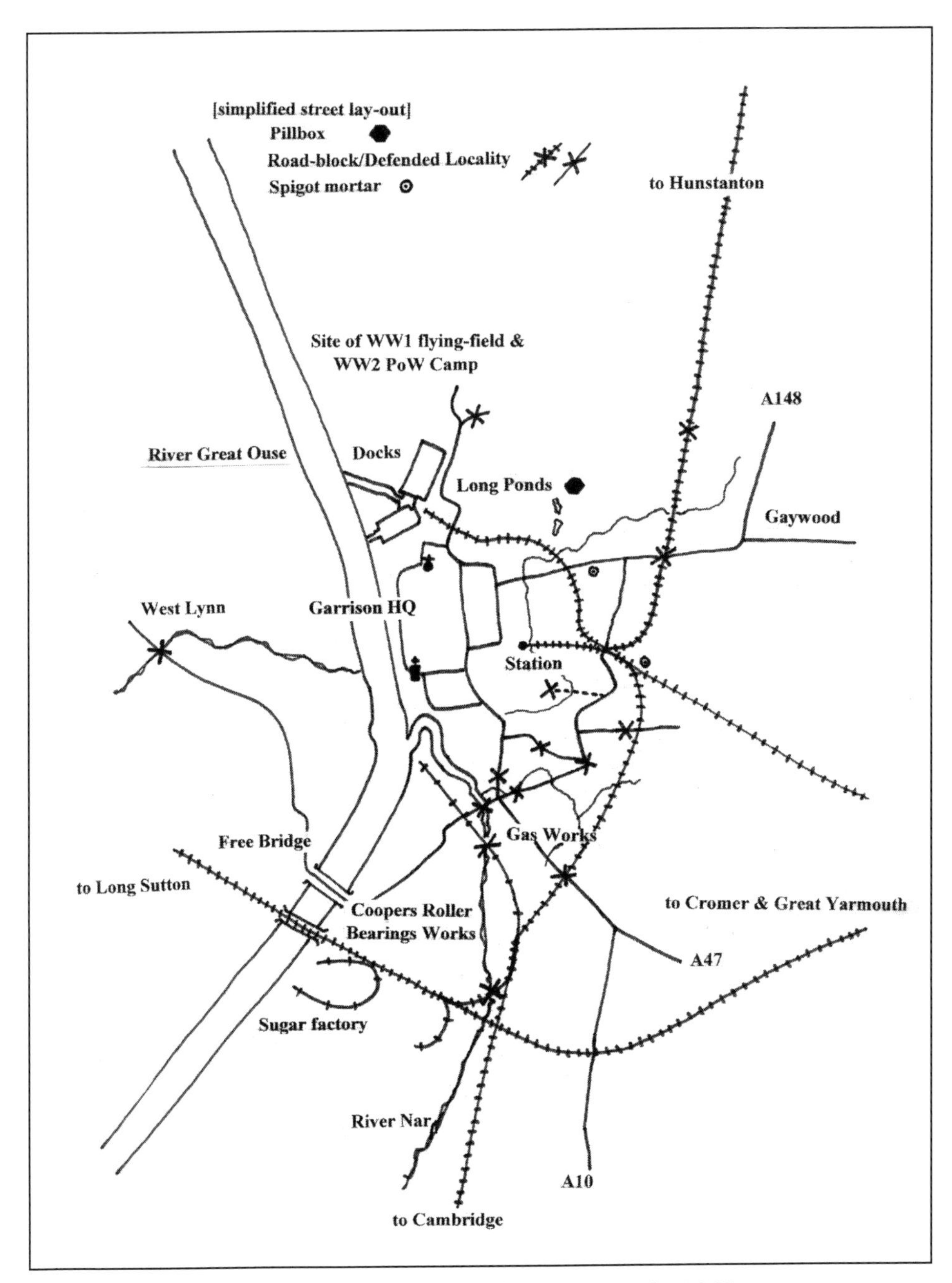

Figure 11 Sketch map to show defences of Kings Lynn in 1941

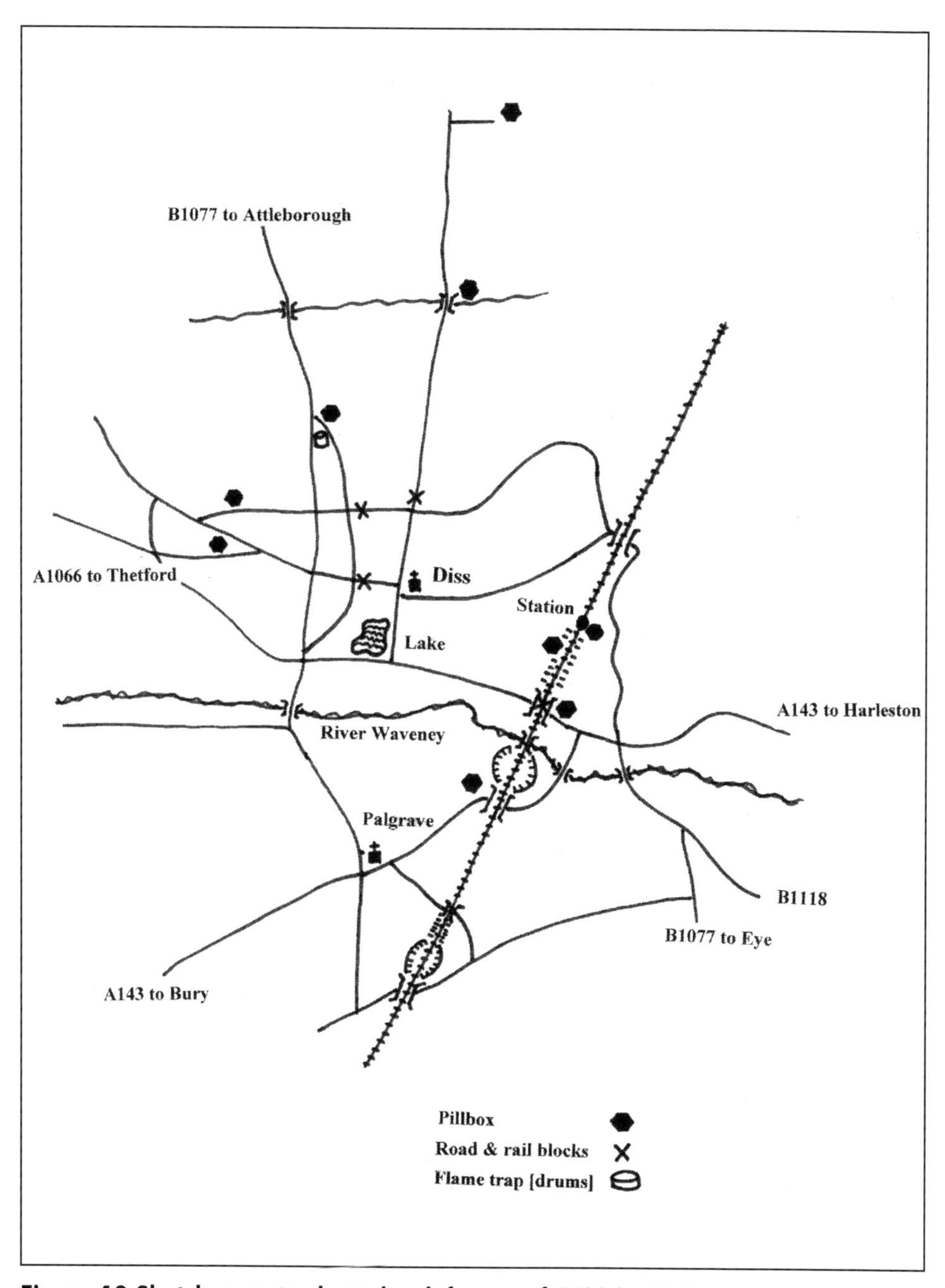

Figure 12 Sketch map to show the defences of DISS in 1941

company and two rifle companies, a section of Bren-gun carriers, and a troop of 18 pounder field-guns. Known as "Norwich Force", it was tasked, as the divisional reserve, with the defence of Aylsham. The four batteries of 125 AT Regiment [RA], a duplicate TA unit from Sunderland, under command of 37 Infantry Bde, were responsible for manning a mixture of 2 pounder and 6 pounder guns, which would be fired from prepared positions. HQ and A & D Batteries were based at Catton Hall, and B & C Batteries at Taverham Hall, Costessey.

Kings Lynn was also designated a Defended Place and given strong defences *[Figure 11]*, owing to its importance both as a port which would have been vital to the enemy's invasion plans, and as the starting-point of two defence lines, one running down the River Great Ouse, linking with the GHQ Line and the Eastern Command Line, and the other crossing Norfolk diagonally through Swaffham, Watton and Harleston. The town's docks, two railway stations and five railway lines, along with the vital A47 east-west road-link from Norwich through to the West Midlands, all contributed to its status as an important communications centre. The town's Invasion Committee was based on the Town Hall, which also served as the combined Battle HQ in the event of invasion. The Defence Scheme was, unsurprisingly focussed on holding the Ouse crossing. The defence was based on the area within a six-mile [9.5km] radius of the town. Lightly-held covering positions, and a network of standing patrols were established to give warning of an enemy approach. A screen of individual or groups of defended buildings, provided positions from which troops in isolated positions such as that at the Sugar Factory, might fall back

54. STRADSETT: a most unusual survival is this spigot mortar spider which would normally be embedded in a thick concrete pedestal [see plate 13].

on the two Keeps, one at the Free Bridge, and the other at the Borough. The town itself, had a garrison provided by 13th Bn. South Staffordshire Regiment in July 1940, with their HQ at 12 Portland Street. Ultimately such units would be supported by two companies of 7th Bn. Norfolk Home Guard, 750 strong, plus another 200 men in a detachment which belonged to the GPO

Home Guard Bn. based in Cambridge, and another company of the CDS Home Guard. The defences were gradually strengthened to include a string of pillboxes forming a semi-circular screen around the east of the town, partly aligned with the railway line to the docks, along which were sited spigot mortar pedestals, with further pillboxes along the river frontage. A ring of road-blocks constructed of AT blocks and rails sealed off the road approaches through West Lynn, with other similar obstructions at the level-crossing on the Gaywood road, and on most of the other roads into town such as Exton Road, London Road at the South Gate, and Goodwins Road. In front of the re-built West Gate, where Broad Walk goes over Rivulet Bridge and through the mediaeval town-walls, there is a grid of sockets set into the ground *[51]*, into which could be inserted hairpins, bent AT rails. There were rail-blocks at Hardwick Bridge, at the bridges over the River Nar, and, to the east of the town station, the junction of three lines which is also covered by a spigot mortar position. Another spigot mortar is located north of the FE College, facing up towards the bridge over the Gaywood River. The MBI was defended by a special purpose platoon which would withdraw to Savages works once the fuel stocks had been destroyed to prevent them falling into the enemy's hands. Another such platoon was tasked with defending the Gaywood Road crossing of the Gaywood River, with orders to fall back and join the reserves at Dodmans Bridge after further resistance was futile. Each of these defended localities plus others at the GPO, South Lynn Station and the Nar Bridge by the Gas Works was defended by roughly platoon-size detachments. Reserves were held at Dodmans Bridge, Coopers Roller-bearing Works, the level-crossing on the Wisbech road, and at The Walks, each group being fifty men. The extent of the Borough Keep included the Custom House, Purfleet Street, High Street, Church Street and Boal Street. The Free Bridge Keep took in Coopers Works.

The defence of nodal points

Most of the towns through which Norfolk's defence lines ran were classed as nodal points, by virtue of their importance in road or rail networks, or as bridging points over the numerous waterways. Two towns which were nodal points, but not on defence lines were Wymondham and Diss. At Wymondham, HQ of the 9th Bn. Norfolk Home Guard, there was an integrated defence plan involving ARP, the Police, and the other civil authorities. This organisation was tested by a mock invasion in September 1942. The Home Guard HQ was at the drill hall in Pople Street, and several areas of the town, including the railway station, were designated as keeps, and these were sealed off by road-blocks. There was an OP in the Abbey tower overlooking the bridge over the River Tiffey, around which, the fixed defences appear to have been grouped. These include two pillboxes and spigot mortars around Cavick House, a sometime searchlight site. Diss *[Figure 12]* had a better-developed system of fixed defences

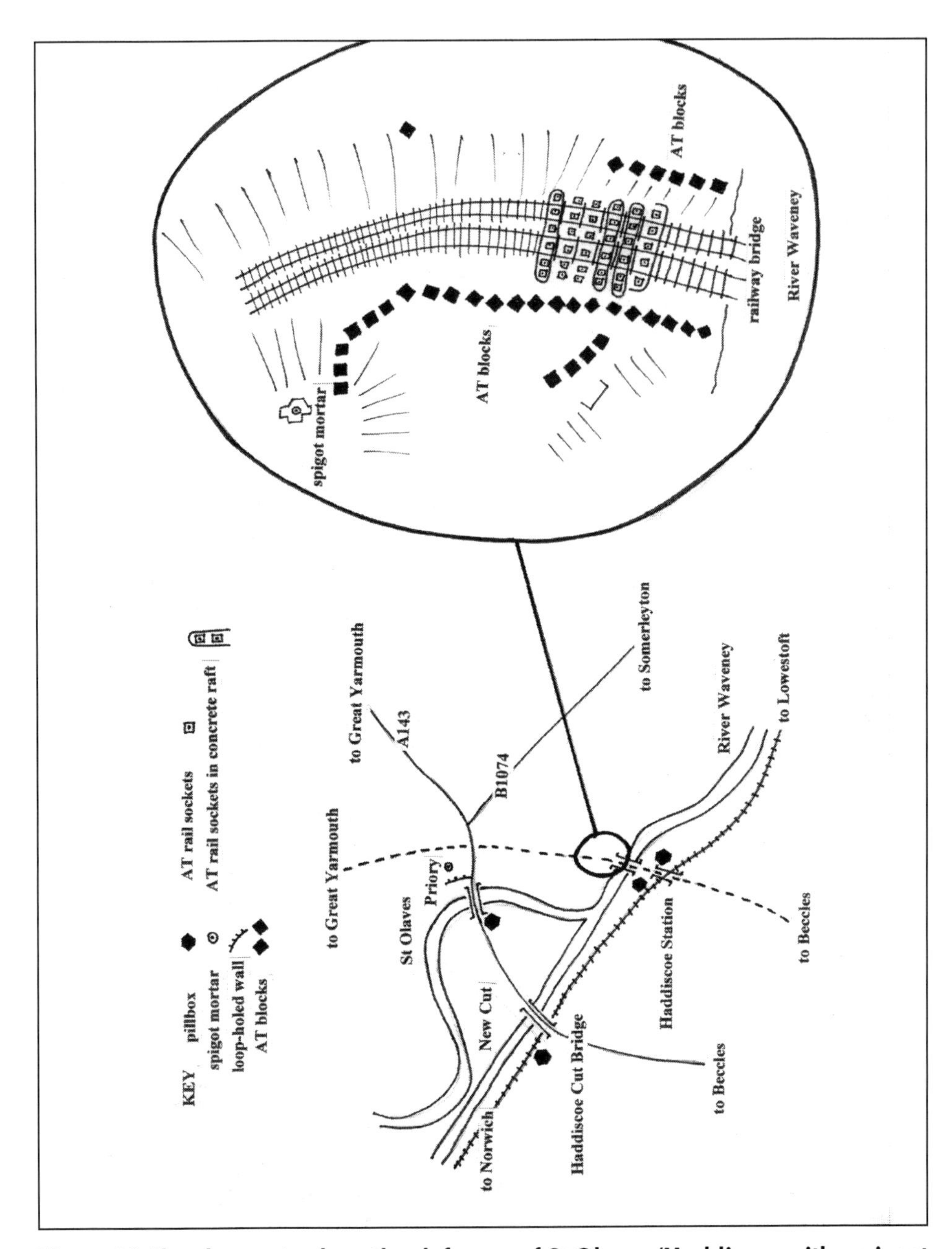

Figure 13 Sketch map to show the defences of St Olaves/Haddiscoe with an inset showing the rail-block north of the river, in detail

55. UPWELL: Home Guard store-house to the usual Norfolk design [TF506026].

56. REEPHAM: 'The Bays', HQ of the local Home Guard contingent.

consisting of at least seven pillboxes, steel rails in sockets blocking the roads out of town and the railway line south of the station, and also a flame fougasse at an important road junction. Initially part of 3rd Bn. Norfolk Home Guard, but later hived off to the new 14th Bn, the Diss company had its HQ in the Royal British Legion club, in Denmark Street, now the Conservative club. Vulnerable points with permanent nightly guards included the water-tower. Shooting practice took place at Wortham Ling, over the county border from Roydon. Both East Dereham, and Swaffham with their important road and rail links were defended by pillboxes *[52]* and spigot mortars.

Of those towns designated nodal points and located on defence lines, after Norwich, Thetford, on the Eastern Command Line, was probably the most heavily fortified. In the north, a group of pillboxes straddle the Croxton road, and another protects the level-crossing on the Watton road at Kilverstone Heath. Closer to the town-centre, several pillboxes and spigot mortars are sited to control access, and an AT emplacement, later converted to a pillbox *[53]*, faces east along the old A11 in the car-park of The Ark PH. There are spigot mortar pedestals west of the priory ruins, at Nuns Bridges and near the Thomas Paine Hotel, the first two at least are the local hexagonal design, that near the priory standing within a raised concrete enclosure. The pillbox on the river bank west of the old town bridge is camouflaged with an outer skin of flint nodules. Another pillbox stands in the allotments near the station. The local Home Guard HQ was Bridge House, the home of the 2i/c. Like Kings Lynn, Great Yarmouth was integrated into the coast defences. It was regarded as the key port on the east coast, so was given maximum defences. The garrison was made up of regular troops, RN personnel, the complements of coast defence and HAA batteries, and 11th Bn. Norfolk Home Guard. Christopher Bird's survey of the area has listed over 100 defence installations, mainly pillboxes, of which around 10% survive. Whilst the sea-front was defended by the three coast defence batteries and all the anti-landing obstacles, usually covered by machine-gun positions and artillery, the land approaches were defended by large numbers of pillboxes. It was a constant concern that enemy troops would avoid a frontal assault in which they must incur heavy losses, and would land north and south of the port, attacking from behind with a pincer movement, and it was against this possibility that the defences were designed.

Defended localities

On a far smaller scale, Thursford is a good example of a village sitting astride important crossroads, and therefore meriting defences. Five roads meet by The Crawfish PH on the Fakenham to Holt road. A defensive perimeter encircled the crossroads with two pillboxes, a spigot mortar, AT blocks, wire, and loopholes cut into the wall behind the pub, all manned by the local Home Guard. A store was provided for ammunition and weapons. Roads were blocked with AT rails, and the main road fitted with trip-wires which triggered a home-made grenade-thrower.

Not only towns and villages constituted nodal points. Quite often important cross-roads out in the country-side merited defences. A good example is that at Stradsett, east of Downham Market *[54]*. Here may be seen two pillboxes, two, originally four spigot mortar mountings, and the remains of an explosives and inflammables store, in this instance, a Nissen hut with a brick dividing-wall. Acle Bridge, some way from the town, was defended by spigot mortars, the pedestals for three of which survive. The important road/rail/river nodal point at St Olaves/Haddiscoe, astride both the River Waveney and F111 defence lines, was heavily-fortified with fixed defences including pillboxes and rail-blocks *[Figure 13]*.

The Norfolk Home Guard

Much of the responsibility for defending all these points fell, as we have seen, to the Home Guard. One of their problems was the lack of tools to do the job, and they developed an alternative armoury of weapons, generally referred to as sub-artillery. One of these weapons was the spigot mortar, or Blacker Bombard, invented pre-War by Major Blacker, and rejected by the War Office. However, its ease and cheapness of manufacture meant that in the changed circumstances of the invasion scare, it suddenly became an attractive proposition. It was tidied up at Winston Churchill's Toy-shop in Buckinghamshire, went into production and began to be issued in 1941, becoming the mainstay of nodal point defence for Home Guard and regular army alike. The mortar fired a 14lb [6.2kg] anti-personnel, or 20lb [8.8kg] anti-tank bomb, with an optimum range of no more than 200 yards. It could be mounted on either permanent or field mountings. The permanent fixture was a steel framework called a spider set into a concrete cylinder, the size of a large oil-drum, with the pintle on top of the spider protruding from the top as a peg for the mortar to sit on. The concrete pedestal sat in a brick-lined pit, with recesses to hold bombs. In low-lying areas, liable to flood, concrete walls were built around the pedestal at ground level. In the Thetford, Brandon and Mildenhall areas, the pedestal is hexagonal in section rather than the normal circular. The pedestals, of which two were meant to be provided for each mortar issued, were built by local contractors. The one standing on Guist Green was one of five constructed by the local builder, himself a member of the Home Guard. The fixed version was ideal for covering such targets as rail and road bridges, where both the range and trajectory could be pre-determined, and it was simply a matter of the crew holding their nerve as a suitable target came into view. The mobile version was quite heavy and cumbersome, with long tubular legs with spade grips for stability, so many Home Guard units, including those in Kings Lynn and Morley, adapted trailers for it. Other examples of sub-artillery were the Northover Projector which fired phosphorus [SIP] grenades, and the 3 inch [75mm] Smith Gun, designed to

57. DOCKING: one of two Norcon pillboxes guarding a Brigade HQ; little more than loop-holed sewer-pipes, these at least have roofs [TF768368].

be towed behind an Austin Seven car. The Smith Gun had solid wheels like dustbin-lids, which doubled as the carriage and turn-table for firing, allowing it to traverse easily. All these weapons and their ammunition were stored in purpose-built explosives and inflammables stores *[55]*. The War Office instruction relating to storage called for strict segregation of the two materials, in two separate stores, and examples can be seen at Docking, Loddon and at Norwich's Thorpe Station. However, many Home Guard detachments had insufficient stores to merit the extravagant use of scarce building materials and labour, so a single store usually sufficed with a brick partition to maintain separation. Examples can be seen at Barnham Beeches, Letheringsett, Upwell and Heacham, amongst many more. The same builder who built spigot mortar pedestals around Guist, built the Home Guard store at Drayton, and commented that it was used to store a Smith Gun, the only one he had ever seen. Sometimes, in the absence of one of these stores, existing buildings were adapted such as the barn in Rectory Road, Coltishall, now "Barn Cottage", a private dwelling. Many Home Guard units adapted civilian vehicles by adding wooden planking and cast-iron or steel armour. The Kings Lynn unit ran a fleet of armoured cars including a 1934 Alvis, three Hillmans, two Fords, a Rover and a Railton. All were fitted with steel plates and anti-grenade screens, and mounted machine-guns.

By 1943, Norfolk had 17 battalions of Home Guard totalling 32 000 men and women. Their HQs occupied a variety of buildings ranging from Melton Constable Hall, home of Lord Hastings, CO of the 4th Bn, to Hall Farm, Hargham, home of the local platoon commander. At Snetterton, the Old Post Office was used, and at Larling, the School House. A number of drill halls such as Wymondham, Reepham, Chapel-fields in Norwich and Aylsham also served as HQs, along with numerous village halls, schools, church halls, pubs and social clubs, and private houses like The Willows in Bawdeswell. Training took place on open spaces, on firing ranges, and for special exercises, in the streets. In Reepham, the HQ of 17th Bn. Norfolk Home Guard was in The Bays *[56]*, a house on Norwich Road, now a private residence. The Bircham Institute, now the Library, was used for lectures and training demonstrations. Also in the Market-place, was a 0.22 inch [5mm] rifle-range in what is now the Function Room of the Old Brewery House Hotel. At Horsford, a full-bore range dating from WWI, was used by the Home Guard and the regular army for rifle shooting and for 0.5 inch [13mm] heavy machine-gun practice. It is still used by the local shooting club. Even a small Home Guard unit had quite extensive requirements in terms of accommodation. In Gorleston, for instance, 1 Platoon of 1 Company of the 11th Bn, had its HQ in a requisitioned, empty private house in Poplar Avenue; held meetings and parades in the [evacuated] Church Road School and another empty house on the Cliffs; used Fellowes Shipyard in Southtown for training; and the rifle-range at Herringfleet for shooting practice. There were sometimes long-term benefits of training exercises, as when the stage and ballet designer, Oliver Messel [1905-1978], by then a captain in the REs, ran a camouflage course in Fakenham, leaving the local Home Guard with a pillbox in the centre of town, masquerading as a classical statue on its plinth. All those who could join the Home Guard did so, from schoolboys, head-hunted by schoolmasters, reared on John Buchan, who recruited them into the Auxiliary Units prior to their call-up proper, through to clergymen, who received official permission [and encouragement] to join from the Bishop of Norwich.

Other vulnerable points

In the early days of the anti-invasion scare, the prioritisation of VPs was quite specific, in order to ensure that the available troops were deployed to best effect. In Operational Instruction No6, issued around May 1940, 55 Infantry Brigade had responsibility for just five VPs: Gorleston Signal Station, Stoke Holy Cross AMES, Pulham bomb-dump, Norwich RAF MU, and Trowse Bridge. As more resources became available, then the list of VPs expanded exponentially. Factories, especially those producing munitions or other commodities important for the war effort very often had their own platoon of the Home Guard, responsible for maintaining a watch against sabotage or espionage, but were otherwise integrated into the general defence plan. Another category of establishment very much more open to attack was the military HQ, particularly those of large formations on coast defence duties. Several Brigade HQs were provided with Allan Williams turrets for their local protection against commando raids aimed at disrupting the command chain. The Allan Williams turret is a revolving steel dome with weapons mountings, which rotates over a sunken chamber entered through a hatch into a short tunnel. It was manned by two soldiers who could rotate the turret manually, as the dome ran on wheels around a track. These were provided at Bayfield Hall near Glandford [3], and at Cockley Cley [4, although nine sites are listed in the Sites & Monuments record]. Docking Hall has two Norcon pillboxes, basically concrete sewer-pipes with four or five loopholes cut in the side. At least here, they have been given domed roofs, but they were usually left open to the sky *[57]*.

In the summer of 1940, as the threat of invasion increased, every possible avenue was explored to impede an invader. Many areas of Norfolk were provided with searchlight cover, and at this stage in the war these lights were given permanent sites in bands across the county. The HQ of 40th AA Brigade at Sawston Hall near Cambridge issued orders that all searchlight sites should have a concrete pillbox as the nucleus of a defensible strong-point with wire and trenches. These strong-points were to be established in consultation with the local "Field Force Commander" and, in the event of an invasion, held until relieved by a unit of the Field Force. There are many instances of these, now isolated, pillboxes across Norfolk, a good example being at Whin Common, Denver, whilst a line of half-a-dozen can be seen at intervals of 3 miles [4.8km] or so between Thetford, through East Harling and Banham to Harleston. These orders, shared with 40 Brigade, appear to have been extended by 41st AA Brigade orders to all AA sites in J Sector, roughly the Norfolk coast in the north, down to a line drawn from Thetford to Diss in the south. Sites were ordered to become self-defensible strong-points within layers of searchlights from the "coastal belts", inland to the" rear belts". Two places, Fakenham and Harleston, were singled out as strong points to be manned by personnel from 65 and 69 Searchlight Regiments respectively. Plans, made in consultation with 2 [sic] Corps, via 18 Division, were to be constantly "checked and rehearsed"

AIRFIELDS IN NORFOLK 3

Although there are records of balloon flights from Norwich as early as around 1800, it was not until the beginning of World War I that military flying became a common activity in Norfolk.

Military aviation in World War I

The Royal Flying Corps' had been founded in 1912, but, as World War I began, the bulk of its strength was deployed with the BEF in France, so the majority of military flying on the home front was controlled by the Admiralty. At Great Yarmouth a Royal Naval Air Station opened in the summer of 1914 catering for both land-based aircraft and sea-planes. What few fighters there were, were operated by the RNAS, with those in Norfolk, being based at Narborough *[58]*. There was also a sea-plane sub-station at Hickling Broad, and a landing-ground at Holt, but possibly the Admiralty's biggest local commitment was still to airships. Supporting the extensive nation-wide naval airship patrol network, there was a large Airship Experimental Station at Pulham, with two enormous sheds *[59]*, and all their associated technical buildings *[60]*. In 1927, Hangar 2 was dismantled and taken for enlargement and re-erection at Cardington in Bedfordshire, where the R100 and R101 Airship project was based. This hangar still stands alongside Cardington's own original. Pulham's remaining Hangar 1 was demolished in 1948.

58. NARBOROUGH: the former World War I Officers' Mess has been re-erected as West Acre village hall [TF779151].

Training stations

Although Norfolk was subsequently found to lie under the flight path of Zeppelins on their bombing raids, it was nevertheless regarded, from early on in the War, as an appropriate location for flying training activities. In 1915, the School of Air Fighting operated at Sedgeford *[61]*, until, in 1916, it was transferred to the newly-opened airfield at neighbouring Bircham Newton. Narborough also had a training function. A site south of Thetford, known as Snarehill Farm or Euston, had been set up in autumn 1915, as a training airfield. It was provided with six hangars and associated workshops and living accommodation, becoming No.4 School of Navigation and Bomb-dropping.

59. PULHAM: the airship hangar moved to Cardington [Bedfordshire] in 1927 as part of the R100 and R101 programme can be seen on the right of this picture.

60. PULHAM: the Silicol building of the World War I airship station.

61. SEDGEFORD: officers' quarters of this World War I airfield.

62. FELTWELL: barrack-blocks dating from World War I.

63. HARLING ROAD: the Aircraft Repair Shed of this Training Depot Station

At the end of 1918 it was closed and the buildings were demolished. Towards the end of World War I, a number of large Training Depot Stations [TDS] were set up across the country including two in Norfolk, at Feltwell *[62]* and at Harling Road *[63]*.

Defending against the Zeppelins

At the beginning of World War I, the very idea of enemy aircraft dropping bombs on mainland Britain had been unimaginable, but the Zeppelin raids on London, beginning in May 1915, necessitated a firm reaction. Initially the RNAS had a responsibility for anti-Zeppelin patrols, with aircraft based at Narborough, Great Yarmouth and Bacton. These aircraft combined with the AA guns and experimental listening devices to counter the threat, but the need for an increased response was marked by the creation of Home Defence [HD] squadrons of fighter-aircraft of the RFC. Each squadron was divided into three flights, each of which was assigned a fully-equipped aerodrome. In Norfolk, 51[HD] Squadron was formed at Norwich in May 1916, with the intention that the three flights would initially be based at Thetford, Mousehold Heath and Narborough. HQ was initially set up as a purely administrative unit at Hingham, with the flights to be based at Harling Road, Mattishall and Narborough, but 'B' Flight was based at Hingham from August 1916. Since it was vital to maintain aircraft in the air for as long as possible, particularly at night, an extensive network of landing-grounds [LG] was established enabling aircraft to stay aloft until their fuel was almost exhausted. In Norfolk, such LGs were laid out at Burgh Castle, Earsham, Freethorpe [near Reedham], Frettenham, Gooderstone, Holt, Marsham, North Elmham, Saxthorpe, Sporle, Tibenham, Tottenhill and West Rudham.. Several of these were specifically equipped for night-time use with Money Flares, braziers of asbestos wool dowsed in paraffin, supplemented by Lyons search-lights and acetylene lamps. These LGs were manned by Defence Corps volunteers who were absorbed into the RAF in 1918. Harling Road airfield was the base from July 1916 for one flight of 51 Home Defence Squadron; the accommodation consisted of a large, timber Aeroplane Shed [130′ x 120′, 40m x 36m], a canvas Bessoneau hangar, and living quarters in wooden huts. By early-1917 these buildings had been augmented by three coupled GS hangars, generally known as Belfast Truss hangars after their mode of roof construction, and an Aircraft Repair Shed. Over the period from then until August 1918, large numbers of workshops, stores, class-rooms, offices and utilities were added, and the living quarters, north of the Roudham Road were also expanded, as there were now three whole squadrons in residence totalling around a thousand personnel. The site was designated No.10 TDS, and operated as such until March 1920.

Anti-U-boat patrols

In 1917, the country was suffering greatly at the hands of U-boats. Patrols were flown from RNAS Great Yarmouth, and other east coast airfields to attempt to disrupt these submarine operations. A number of methods were used to get observers into the skies to increase the visible range of these patrols. Kite Balloons attached by cables to destroyers were towed along patrol lanes; Submarine Scouts were small rigid airships with the fuselage of a BE2 slung underneath; and Felixstowe F2A flying boats were also used. A patrol grid known as the Spiders Web was notionally drawn using the North Hinder lightship as the centre-point, from which radiated eight arms 30 miles [48km] long. Lines linking these radial arms, ten and twenty miles [16 and 32 km] from the central point created a web of 24 sections in the eight sectors. Two sectors could be over-flown in a five-hour-long patrol, visiting each of the six sections twice.

64. BIRCHAM NEWTON: these huts stood alongside the World War I Officers' Mess before its replacement by later buildings.

Whilst no U-boats were actually sunk by this approach, it did keep them submerged and otherwise occupied.

The first heavy bombers

Hingham was the venue for the formation of the RFC's first night-bomber squadron which shortly moved to Farnborough [Hampshire]. The success of the German

65. BIRCHAM NEWTON: the double squash courts [2078/18].

bombing campaign, though condemned on moral grounds, was still seen as a potentially successful strategic weapon, and moves towards gaining the means to pursue a bombing offensive on the German homeland were promoted. As it happened, these ambitions were to be overtaken by events, but not before the enormous Handley-Page V/1500 four-engined heavy bomber, a bi-plane with a wingspan of 126' [38.4m], had been developed. In June 1918, Bircham Newton *[64]* became home to 166 and 274 Squadrons RAF, tasked with carrying out the first such missions. Although these first steps in strategic bombing were never carried through, a Norfolk airfield had, for better or worse, been instrumental in the development of the concept of the independent bombing force within the newly-established RAF.

The development of military airfields between the wars; the Expansion Period

The relief which followed the Armistice of 1918 and the apparent security offered by the Treaty of Versailles, coupled with an empty treasury, ensured that Britain's armed

66. BIRCHAM NEWTON: barrack blocks, to drawing number 1100/28 on the left, and to 2537/36 on the right.

forces would be run down. The RAF had ended the War with over 20 000 aircraft but immediate reductions in both machines and personnel led to ten years of struggle to maintain any sort of viable service. A succession of plans was rolled out throughout the 1920s, aimed at producing maximum effectiveness for minimal expenditure. A very limited expansion in 1923-4, sought to restore the basic

67. WATTON: the 'Fort' type watch office [207/36], the concrete version of that at Bircham Newton in brick [1959/34].

foundations on which the RAF might expand, by establishing permanent specialist airfields, their structures and organisation designed for purpose. One of these eight was in Norfolk- a re-furbished Bircham Newton, once more designed as a base for heavy bombers. The skeleton of the airfield as it stood in 1918, had, unlike some airfields where instant demolition had occurred, fortunately survived. The three coupled GS hangars, the ARS, stores and workshops were all brought back into service, but complemented by new structures such as the smart new guardhouse to a design of 1923, the vital squash courts *[65]* without which no RAF station could possibly be complete and over time, new barrack blocks *[66]*, permanent and brick-built, with more than a nod towards elegance, with their neo-Georgian pediments, and their creature comforts.

The basis of much of this 1920s planning was an assumption that bomber stations belonged in the Thames Valley, and fighter stations should ring London. By 1934, however, Germany was beginning to re-arm, and defensive orientation had to be realigned. The next tranche of new airfields would be facing the North Sea. Included in this 1934 building programme were new bomber bases at Feltwell and Marham, both having been airfields in World War I. The 1937 Scheme included Watton and West Raynham as new bomber bases, and provided another make-over for Bircham Newton, whose 1917 GS hangars were exchanged for the new 'C' Type ones. New

68. WEST RAYNHAM: 'Fort' type Watch Office [207/36] with later adaptations [4698/43].

messes for officers, for sergeants and for airmen were provided, as were new administrative and medical facilities. A 'Fort' watch office to a design of 1934 also

69. COLTISHALL: Hangar 3, one of the four 'C' type [2029/34] remaining from the late 1930s airfield.

70. COLTISHALL: the 'Villa' type Watch Office [2328/39] the concrete version [as at Horsham St Faith] of Swanton Morley's in brick [5845/39].

71. SWANTON MORLEY: the 'Villa' type watch office [5845/39] [photo AGK].

72. WEST RAYNHAM: Main Stores [4287/35] the concrete version of Bircham Newton's in brick [7064/37].

73. WEST RAYNHAM: Officers' Mess [2948/34].

appeared, replacing the control-top, a cabin perched on a corner of the middle GS hangar, and overlooking the flying field. At the same time, the station was transferred from Bomber Command to Coastal Command. Other airfields provided with 'Fort' type watch offices at this time were Marham, Watton *[67]* and West Raynham *[68]*. A further, post-Munich, Scheme

74. WATTON: Main Workshops [4923/35] the concrete version of Bircham Newton's in brick [1354/38].

provided new fighter stations at Coltishall and at Horsham St Faith, originally conceived as a satellite of Watton.

The recognition that East Anglia might well be in the front line in any imminent conflict meant that whole categories of airfield-Aircraft Storage Units, Armament Training Camps, and much of the flying training establishment were sited further west and

75. HORSHAM ST FAITH: Station HQ [1723/36].

north, leaving Norfolk to host mainly operational units. All these airfields were built to a similar compact plan using uniform building types, in a clean-lined, neo-Georgian style, influenced by Sir Edwin Lutyens, and approved by the Royal Fine Arts Commission and the Council for the Preservation of Rural England. These designs came out of the Air Ministry Works Department, and were universally applied. Thus one can easily recognise building functions at all these airfields simply by looking at the structure itself, or even the footprint on a ground-plan. The hangars were built in a curve to provide some protection from a stick of bombs. Many buildings had protected roofs filled with layers of sand, were camouflaged, and were provided with blast-walls and earth

76. SWANTON MORLEY: T2 hangar, used by commercial flyers [TG001194].

traverses. Many airfields had elegant art deco watch offices, often referred to as 'Villa' type, with wrap-around, metal-framed windows. Both Coltishall *[69 & 70]* and Horsham St Faith were given 'Villas' and C-type hangars. The final group of Expansion Period airfields announced in 1939, included the fighter station of Swanton Morley. Stations in this group were sometimes built to compromise designs. Whereas many of the buildings could be the same as those in earlier schemes, some of the 1939-40 airfields were given a less elegant watch office [518/40] and less substantial J-type hangars, which were easier and faster to build, and were more economical in materials than the standard C-type. Interestingly, Swanton Morley *[71]* got its 'Villa' [5845/39] but has a J-type hangar [5836/39]. At all these airfields, all the key structures, such as stores *[72]*, messes *[73]*, workshops *[74]* and administrative buildings *[75]* were built to the same high standard either in brick or in concrete.

Military airfields in World War II

Despite so many new airfields coming into service either side of the outbreak of war, there was to be an almost insatiable demand for still more throughout the duration. The Expansion Period airfields had conformed to peace-time requirements for aesthetically pleasing construction, and a sympathetic relationship with the landscape. The priorities and realities of

77. FOULSHAM: one of several T2 hangars here, caught in the process of re-cladding. This transportable hangar was designed to be moved around so the structure was relatively easily dismantled and re-erected [witness the T2 at the top end of Hethel for instance which was imported in the 1970s].

war, however meant that an entirely different type of airfield was needed. There would be two major differences. The compact design of 1930s airfields may have lessened the impact on the landscape, and reflected the order and neatness typically demanded by even this most junior of armed services, but it did little to lessen the effect of enemy bombing. Thus the new airfields would be characterised by the dispersal of aircraft into

78. THORPE ABBOTTS: the Watch Office [13726/41] designed for bomber satellite stations.

remote hangars, pens and hard-standings, and of personnel into scattered enclaves of living quarters known as Communal Sites. The imposing neo-Georgian buildings would be exchanged for utility structures, mainly in temporary brick [tb], single-thickness brick walls, strengthened by buttresses, and rendered in cement; Nissen huts, invented by a Canadian engineer officer in World War I, and their derivatives:

79. LUDHAM: the Watch Office [3156/41] designed for fighter satellite stations, and superseded by the 343/43 which stands alongside.

Romney and Iris huts; or a wide range of other huts constructed out of concrete panels, plaster-board, asbestos sheet, or timber. For the substantial, and hopefully permanent, 'C' type hangars, were substituted the flimsier Bellman [8349/37] and, later on, the T1, T2 *[76 & 77]* and T3 [T for 'transportable]. These came in pre-fabricated form, as did many of the hut-types, and could be erected relatively quickly on concrete bases. An aircraft repair hangar, the B1, was developed by the Ministry of Aircraft Production [MAP] to house on-site repair and maintenance operations aimed at keeping airworthy as many aircraft as possible.

In contrast to the luxury and solidity of pre-war watch offices, a range of utility types was developed for specific airfield functions, followed by a generic version which fulfilled the needs of all types of airfield. Three Norfolk airfields-Foulsham, Hardwick and Shipdham, opened in mid-1942 with the stop-gap 518/40 watch office, but all the other wartime starts were given either a specialist tower, or the generic version [12779/41 or 343/43]. Some Bomber Satellite stations and Operational Training Units [OTU] received Type 13726/41 watch offices as at Sculthorpe, Seething and Thorpe Abbotts *[78]*. Sometimes, an earlier watch office was replaced by the generic one. Thus Ludham *[79]* and Matlaske had watch offices suitable for Fighter Satellite stations [respectively 3156/41 and 18441/40] and both ended up with 343/43s. Docking, Oulton and Bodney had their Bomber Satellite watch offices [15898/40] replaced with 343/43s for different reasons. Docking's and Oulton's, because they were no longer fit for purpose,

80. WATTON: one of the arc of four 'C' type hangars which have recently [2008] been demolished.

and Bodney's, because one of its pilots marked D-Day by demolishing it. 'Forts' such as Watton's were generally replaced, in this case by a 12779/41. Many of the Bomber Satellites had single-storey Type A [17821/40] watch offices, as at Attlebridge, or Type B [7345/41] as at Tibenham. Rather

81. NORTH CREAKE: Main Stores consisting of two Romney huts linked by a hut in temporary brick.

than building a complete new watch office, an observation floor [13079/41] was added above the ground-floor control room, to most of these types, as at Downham Market and Great Massingham. Those airfields which were built later in the war, generally received a Type 343/43 watch office to start with. Examples in Norfolk include Deopham Green, Langham, Little Snoring, North Creake, Rackheath, Snetterton Heath and Swannington.

The standard allocation of hangars to wartime bomber airfields was three T2s, early in the war as at Hardwick and Hethel, but soon reduced to two T2s, as at, for example, Deopham Green, Old Buckenham, Thorpe Abbotts and Wendling. To these was often added, between 1942 and 1944, one B1 MAP hangar, as at North Creake and Swannington. Several Norfolk bomber airfields were provided with an extra two or three T2s specifically for the storage of gliders, examples being Downham Market [3], Great Massingham [2], Little Snoring [2], and Swanton Morley [3]. Some airfields ended up with large numbers of hangars for different purposes. Foulsham had its standard two T2s and single B1, but three more T2s for glider storage, and a further four T2s to carry out its function as a Base Major Maintenance Section. Watton had four Expansion Period 'C' type hangars *[80]*, to which were added three T2s and two B1s, presumably as part of the adjoining Neaton depot site. East Wretham was one of several airfields opened as satellites, and, initially not

82. NORTH CREAKE: only the projection-room end of the cinema survives here, the Nissen auditorium has been removed.

83. SWANNINGTON: the classic combination of Tractor and Trailer Shed, Fire Tender Shed [Nissen] and Watch Office [343/43] can be seen here.

provided with hangars at all. Eventually, when it was switched from bombers to fighters in 1943, it was given two Bellmans, possibly re-deployed from another airfield with less need of them. Bircham Newton also supplemented its three 'C' type hangars with three Bellmans. Many fighter stations had no large hangars, finding it safer to disperse aircraft around the airfield perimeter either in fighter pens protected by earth traverses, or in low, easily-hidden Blister hangars.

In the same way that the airfields' signature buildings were reduced to a more utilitarian style, so, too, were the more mundane canteens and messes, stores and workshops, offices and living quarters. All these buildings were built to standard Air Ministry designs, but either in temporary brick, or made up of different combinations of huts and sheds. Thus the wartime versions of the Main Stores or Main Workshops tended to be a pair of Romneys or 24' Nissens linked by a tb lobby and offices, as can be seen at North Creake *[81]*, Fersfield and Oulton, for instance [5851 and 5852/42], or at Bodney [826 & 827/43]. One building put up on most airfields, whether established or emergency is the Gymnasium [14604 or 16428/40], often with extensions for either Chapel [15424/41] or Cinema [8891/42] examples of which can be seen at North Creake *[82]*, Methwold, Watton, Hethel, Deopham Green and Great Massingham. If not actually modular, it would appear that attempts were made to simplify designs to make certain structures inter-changeable. At Swannington, for instance, the NFE Store and the Tractor and Trailer Shed share a drawing number [12411/41, even though they appear quite different structures *[83]*.

84. WEST RAYNHAM: a new Control Tower for a new era; this post-war 294/45 was provided to cater for the station's new roles.

The wartime airfield construction programme was enormous, peaking in 1942 when one third of the nation's construction workers were employed on it. It took 11000 labourers, on average five to seven months to build the basic infra-structure, with completion in eighteen months, and, throughout 1942, a new airfield was opening somewhere in Britain every three days. As well as taking over new and established airfields from the RAF, the USAAF needed fifty new airfields from scratch, of which 36 were built by the Air Ministry. In Norfolk, the 8th USAAF took over two established RAF stations, four newly-built ones, and were given ten new airfields specifically built for their sole use. If the impact of all these new airfields on the country as a whole was significant, at a local level it must have been overwhelming. Tiny villages suddenly found themselves with the equivalent of a small town springing up on their doorstep, given that the complement of the average bomber base was a little under 3000 service personnel.

In order to make it possible for bomber pilots to make safer landings in foggy weather, the FIDO system was developed. Pierced pipes were laid alongside the runway through which petrol flowed being ignited to heat the air and so disperse the fog. The system had its first working trial at Downham Market, and was then installed at Foulsham as well. In neighbouring Suffolk, Tuddenham and Woodbridge also had FIDO, and, additionally, the latter airfield was provided with an extra-long and extra-wide runway, on which damaged aircraft heading for East Anglian airfields, might be landed. Air-sea rescue craft, manned by both RN and RAF personnel, were based at Gorleston, Felixstowe and Lowestoft.

In addition to fully-developed airfields, there were also simple landing-strips to meet a number of differing needs. Both army and RAF HQs needed the facility to fly in plans, messages or personnel in a hurry, so airstrips served Bylaugh Hall [TF035158] and Costessey. Hemsby's strip was for Army Co-operation Lysanders in 1940 [TG478177]. A strip at Heigham Homes [TG441205] was used for clandestine flights, probably connected with SOE operations.

Military airfields in the Cold War: 1945-89

Towards the end of World War II there had been plans to up-grade a number of airfields to accommodate the increasingly large types of heavy bomber then under development. Both Marham and Sculthorpe were chosen to be such bases and accordingly were provided with new, longer runways. Each had one of 3000 yards and two of 2000 yards, all of them measuring 250 yards across. Part of the general improvement was the provision of a new Control Tower, the 294/45 design for very heavy bomber stations. At the same time, West Raynham was provided with one of these towers *[84]* whilst retaining its original runways- the longest being 2000 yards. It then became the Central Fighter Establishment until 1960, when it resumed its role as an operational fighter station until 1975. Apart from the new control towers, most of the reconstruction had gone into providing large areas of concrete hard-standing, 10"-12" [25-30cm.] in depth. In 1948, Sculthorpe, its re-fit completed, re-opened as an American bomber base equipped with B-29s, later replaced by B50s, B-45 jet bombers, and tanker aircraft for aerial re-fuelling. Although these active operations continued only into the 1960s, the base remained on a stand-by status for some time. Marham re-opened after its post-war refit as the Central Bomber Establishment, then trained air-crew converting to US B-29 Washingtons. It also accommodated a USAF bomber group of thirty aircraft of Strategic Air Command. By

1954 resident operational RAF squadrons were equipped with Canberras, and, two years later, with Valiant V-bombers. In 1958 it became the main base for tankers, its Victors operational through the Falklands War and beyond. From 1983, Tornados were based at Marham, and more recently, Harriers. Large numbers of Hardened Aircraft Shelters [HAS] have been built to accommodate these aircraft *[85]*. During Marham's time as a V-bomber base, provision was made at Coltishall for two of its aircraft to be dispersed there. Coltishall itself operated as a fighter base into the new millennium, retaining its original 'Villa' watch office [2328/39] all that time.

As well as the aircraft-delivered H-bomb, based in part, as we have seen, at Marham, Britain's nuclear deterrent was supplemented by the Inter-mediate Range Ballistic Missile THOR, under joint British and US control. There were four groups of these missile sites on the eastern side of England, with the most southerly one based in East Anglia. The main site for the group was at Feltwell, which was also the main training centre for THOR, with another subsidiary site at North Pickenham. The other sites in the group were at Mepal in Cambridgeshire, and at Shepherds Grove and Tuddenham in Suffolk. Each site held three THOR rockets, kept on long canvas-covered trailers, which could be raised by means of a gantry into the vertical firing-position. Thick concrete L-shaped blast-walls protected the crew and the sensitive services from the blast. The missile had a range of 1500 miles [2400 km], and was a stop-gap until a longer-range ICBM could be developed. Hence this system remained in commission for only a very short time between September 1958 and July 1963. At Feltwell, one of the pre-War 'C' type hangars was converted into a receipt, inspection & maintenance [RIM] building for the missiles. Another hangar was used as a technical storage building, and a third hangar contained a launcher-erector for training. Feltwell's THOR structures lie under the golf-course and in the shadow of the space surveillance golf-balls. The blast-walls now appear also to have gone from North Pickenham.

Norfolk's military airfields: a gazetteer *[Figure 14]*

NB: Alternative names for airfields are shown in brackets; USAAF airfield designation is shown, where applicable, in brackets immediately after the airfield name; Air Ministry drawing-numbers for building designs are numbered in the order in which they were produced, followed by the year: thus drawing number 343/43 for the Watch Office for all Commands was the 343rd drawing to emerge from the Air Ministry in 1943.

1 **ATTLEBRIDGE** [Station 120] Opened in 1941 as a satellite of Swanton Morley with light bomber. It was taken over by USAAF in 1942 operating Marauders and later, Liberators. It was used by Maintenance Command from 1945 until 1959. Surviving structures include: the Type A Watch Office

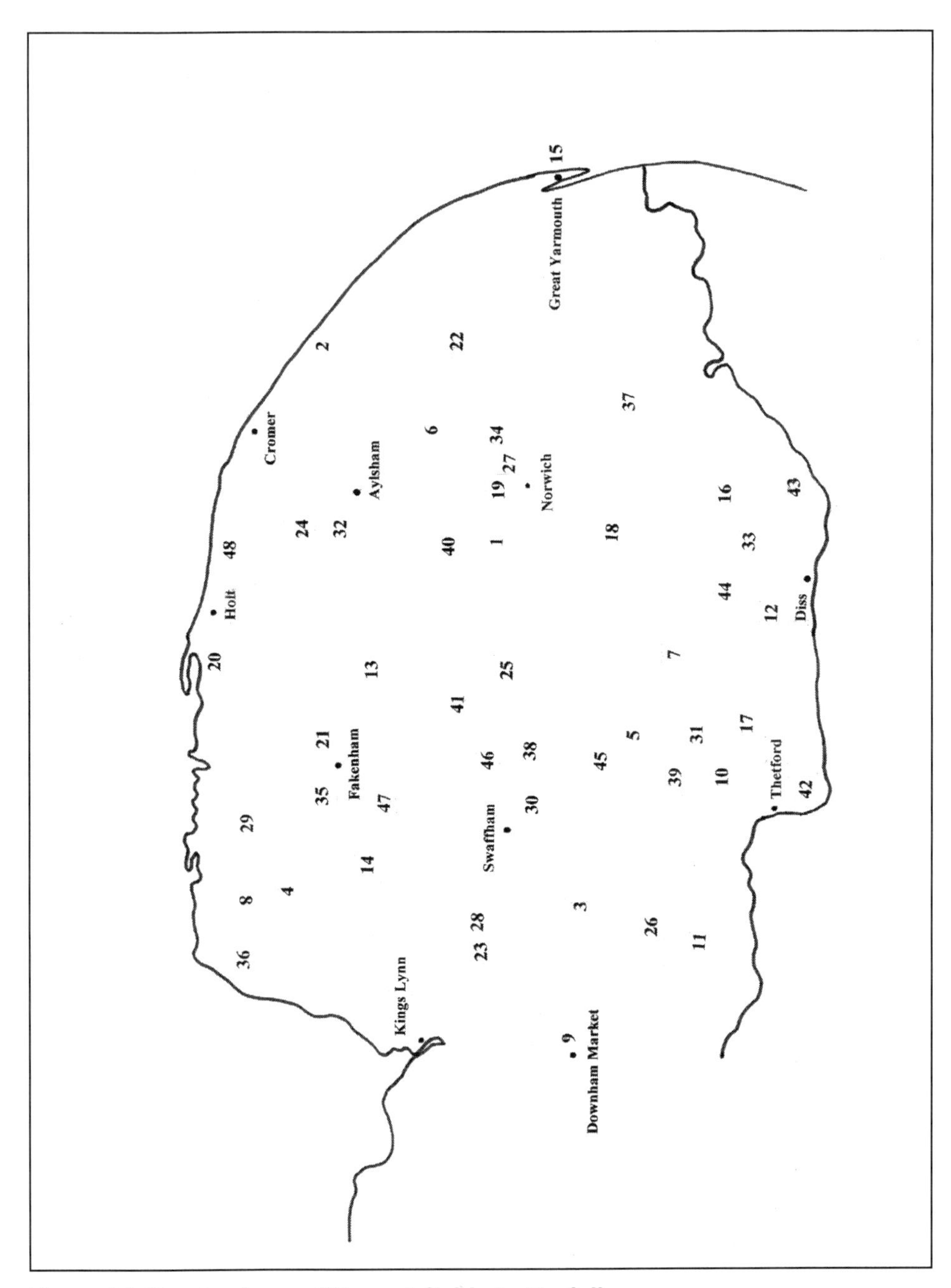

Figure 14 Map to show military airfields in Norfolk

85. MARHAM: Hardened Aircraft Shelter [HAS] provided for fighter-bombers.

86. BIRCHAM NEWTON: the boiler-house and pump-house [694/23] of the post-World War I refurbishment.

87. BIRCHAM NEWTON: the Station Commander's house of c1924.

88. BODNEY: the Watch Office [343/43] built in 1944 to replace the earlier one [18898/40] demolished on D-Day in a flying accident.

89. BODNEY: a Braithwaite tank [20/40] holding 30000 gallons and pump-house.

for bomber satellites, with added observation room and extended control room is reported as being recently demolished, but the Operations Block survives as does an Armoury [17824/40].

2 **BACTON** was operated as a RNAS fighter station against the Zeppelin raids from early 1915; two aircraft sheds were supplied by Boulton and Paul, but facilities were generally rudimentary; it was close to Broomholm Priory.

3 **BARTON BENDISH** was used as a makeshift satellite of Marham being replaced by Downham Market in 1942 as it was unsuitable for Stirlings, and few traces survive.

4 **BIRCHAM NEWTON** Opened in 1916 as a Fighter School, converting to heavy bombing in 1918 but was overtaken by the Armistice. It re-opened as a heavy bomber station but re-organised and rebuilt as a Coastal Command base in 1936,

90. BODNEY: Main Workshops and Main Stores in Romney huts [826-7/43].

91. COLTISHALL: Link Trainer building [12386/38].

operating throughout WWII in a variety of roles including convoy protection, meteorological reconnaissance, air-sea rescue, bombing, escort duties, anti-submarine patrols, and army co-operation, particularly in connection with Weybourne AA Camp. There then followed a largely training function until closure at end of 1962. It is now the Construction Industry Training Centre and largely complete with buildings from all the building periods.

92. COLTISHALL: Institute/dining-room for other ranks [1482-4/36] unchanged apart from the new pitched roof.

Surviving structures include: Watch Office [1959/34], three 'C' type hangars [2029/34]; three Bellman hangars [8349/37]; Station HQ [1725/36]; Officers'

93. COLTISHALL: Fighter pens from the days of the Hurricane, constructed of concrete sandbags.

Mess [2948/34]; Sergeants' Mess [3484/36]; Guard-house & Fire Party [166/23]; Power-house [624/23] *[86]*; Squash Court [2078/18]; Barrack blocks Type L [1132/38 and 11587/38] and Type C [1100/28]; Airmen's Mess and NAAFI

94. COLTISHALL: blast-walls built for the Lightnings, and later, the Jaguars which were based here.

[1483/36]; CO's house *[87]*and Parachute Store [175/36];

5 **BODNEY** [Station 141] Opened early-1940 as satellite of Watton, and operated night intruder raids until May 1943 when it was taken over by USAAF fighters. The original watch-office [15898/40] was accidentally demolished by a Mustang on D-Day, and replaced by the present tower [343/43]. It closed in 1945. It had two T2 hangars and five Blisters. Surviving structures include: Watch Office *[88]* and associated NFE Store and Floodlight Tractor and Trailer shed, water tower and pump-house *[89]*, the Flight Workshop [Bdg.181], Main Stores and Main Workshops *[90]*, latrines and shelters.

6 **COLTISHALL** [Station 355] Begun early-1939 as a bomber base, but switched to fighters and was used by them throughout WWII. Allocated to USAAF but rescinded as RAF needed the base for night-fighters. Offsite Operations Rooms dating from around 1940 were established at Stratton Strawless Hall just off the A140, and at RAF Old Catton. In 1958, it was extensively refurbished and given blast-walled hard-standings for fighter aircraft [29]. Until its closure it was synonymous with the Jaguar, having comprehensive support facilities which continued in use into the new Millennium. It closed in 2006 and, as of 2008, is planned as a Category 'C' prison. Surviving structures include: Watch Office [2328/39]; four 'C' type hangars [2029/34]; and the majority of the 1930s

95. DEOPHAM GREEN: a Transformer Enclosure on Communal Site 4, next to the Gymnasium/chapel.

airfield *[91-94]*, plus all the more recent workshops and stores, engine-testing facilities, flight simulator, guided missile storage etc.

7 **DEOPHAM GREEN** [Station 141] Was in use by USAAF bombers from early-1944 to the end of WWII when RAF Maintenance Command occupied it until 1959. It had two T2 hangars and a watch office [343/43]. Surviving structures include: the Gymnasium/chapel and a stand-by set house *[95]* on Site 4, a Nissen hut, formerly the base library now a carpentry workshop, and some living-huts on Site 7. The only apparent survival on the main site would appear to be the pump-house

8 **DOCKING** Opened in July 1940 as a satellite of Bircham Newton, flying anti-shipping patrols, air-sea rescue and meteorological reconnaissance missions. It was relinquished by Coastal Command in 1945, and finally sold off in 1959. It had one T2 hangar, described on the airfield plan as being used by MAP personnel, and eight Extra Over Blister hangars. Its original watch office [15898/40 Type A for bomber satellites] was replaced with a new one [12779/41 or 343/43] for no obvious reason other than refurbishment. Surviving structures include: Watch Office [12779/41]; parts of Communal site including a de-contamination centre [13843/40] and stand-by set house

96. DOCKING: a Handcraft hut on an AA site.

[12613/40]; BCF and Handcraft huts *[96]* on a Bofors LAA site [BCF/32/11 and 2996/41]; AMWD Tractor Store [WA7/287/41]; Agricultural Plant Store [WA7/121/41].

9 **DOWNHAM MARKET** Opened as a satellite of Marham from 1942 replacing Barton Bendish, operating Stirlings and later, Mosquitos both as bombers and as Pathfinders. It closed in 1946 and was sold ten years later. Officially it had five T2 hangars, three of which were for glider storage, and a single B1, although an aerial photograph taken in 1946 clearly shows

seven hangars. It had a watch office [7345/41 Type B for bomber satellites plus an observation room to 13079/41]. The Officers' Mess was in the Old Rectory next to Bexwell Church. In October 1943, FIDO was installed, this being only the second operational station to receive the system. Surviving structures include: tb guardroom and other huts, Romney hut and Blister hangar all on Technical Site; mess and dining-room on dispersed communal site;

97. EAST WRETHAM: the Operations Block with adjacent Crew-briefing room in the Nissen hut.

10 **EAST WRETHAM** [Station 133] Opened as a satellite of Honington and later of Mildenhall operating Wellingtons. In late-1943 the fighters of USAAF moved in, staying until late 1945. It had two Bellman [8349/37] hangars, plus six Blisters and a canvas structure with a steel frame. It had a Type A watch office for bomber satellites [15898/40] with structural modifications to strengthen the operations room [to 7344/41], possibly as preparation for adding a central observation room on top. Much of the land was sold, but some is retained by the MOD as part of the Stanford Battle-training Area. Surviving structures include: a Bellman hangar and the Operations block with Nissen crew-briefing room alongside *[97]*;

11 **FELTWELL** Began life in World War I as No.7 Training Depot Station with provision similar to that at Harling Road, but was closed after the end of the War. Then it re-opened in April 1937 as a heavy bomber base flying Wellingtons, and, after that, as the Bomber Development Unit testing new aircraft, equipment and techniques, operating alongside a Lancaster training unit. After 1945 more flying-training units were based here but flying ceased in 1958. It was chosen as the centre of the THOR IRBM system in East Anglia, and of national training on the THOR system. It remains in service by listeners with their large golf-balls, and in the 1980s was a USAF emergency stores and hospital. Its layout as a TDS included the usual three double GS hangars, each with a small shed as a flight office, and a smaller ARS. Huts housing workshops, stores, living quarters and instructional class-rooms, and more substantial officers' mess and institute completed the set-up. Between 1935-37 it was completely rebuilt as a two-squadron bomber station with five 'C' type hangars, a 'Fort' type watch office [1959-60/34], and all the associated buildings of an Expansion Period airfield. Essentially this lay-out survives, having seen the THOR launch emplacements come and go, and the

construction of the space surveillance installations. Surviving structures include: most of the 1930s buildings including five 'C' type hangars; the intact WWII bomb-stores; the airfield also houses a school for the children of US personnel, in refurbished 1935 barrack-blocks. On the Brandon Road is a collection of seven World War 1 barrack-huts, the only remaining vestiges of the TDS, later used as living accommodation by local people avoiding the flooding which affected the area, along with a general housing shortage at the end of World War II.

98. FERSFIELD: a pair of Romney huts forming the Main Workshops [5851/42].

12 **FERSFIELD** [Winfarthing][Station 554 ex-140] Opened in August 1942 as USAAF bomber base operating until November 1944 when RAF moved in.Under the control of Knettishall [Suffolk], it hosted Operation Aphrodite, which involved radio-controlled ageing bombers, packed with 20 000lb [9 000kg] of explosive, being steered remotely by accompanying fighters over continental targets, but with little success. The airfield had two T2 hangars and a watch office [343/43]. Surviving structures include: Main Stores and Main Workshops in paired Romney huts *[98]* Ops Block, a T2 hangar and Gas Clothing & Respirator Store [13730/41].

13 **FOULSHAM** [Station B-13] Opened in mid-1942 for RAF Mitchell-equipped squadrons. Its allocation to USAAF was rescinded and only small detachments served here. It hosted intelligence-gathering units, but, under care and maintenance from 1945-1955, a USAF signals unit was based there. The airfield had nine T2 hangars and a single B1, and a watch office [518/40]. Foulsham was one of only two Norfolk airfields to be equipped with FIDO, the petrol-fired fog dispersal system. Fuel for this was stored in large steel tanks encased in brick. Surviving structures include: several of the hangars including one recently stripped to the frame and re-clad, and one or two other buildings including the Tractor & Trailer Shed.

14 **GREAT MASSINGHAM** Opened summer 1940 as a satellite of West Raynham, operating first Blenheims, then Bostons. Later the Bomber Support Training Unit was in residence, followed by Mosquito night-fighters. Following only sporadic use by West Raynham, the airfield was sold in 1958. It had four T2 hangars and a single B1. Its watch office appears to have been an amalgam of Types A and B for bomber satellites. Possibly it had the general layout of Type A [15898/40] subsequently coupled

99. GREAT MASSINGHAM: Free Gunnery Trainer in a Blister hangar [7316/42].

with a Type B watch office and operations room [7345/41], other modifications [13079/41 & 4170/43] affecting the final form of the control room which may have been expanded from the earlier observation room. A plan of 1944 refers merely to the Type A watch office with attached crew-briefing room. Surviving structures include: a Braithwaite tank, a T2 hangar [3657/42], and the Free Gunnery Trainer *[99]* in a Blister hangar [7316/42]. On a detached communal site are a Gymnasium/chapel, a squash court, a dining-room and several other huts.

15 **GREAT YARMOUTH** Opened in April 1913 as a Royal Naval Air Station operating both sea-planes, and conventional aircraft, and carrying out anti-shipping and anti-Zeppelin patrols prior to the RFC's assumption of that role. It appears to have been provided with two F-sheds, another large double hangar, and several Besonneau hangars, all in line parallel to the shore, where there were two jetties to serve the float-planes. The flying-field lay between the hangar-line and the River Yare. As a RAF station it continued until 1920. Its site now lies under a former caravan-park, a Power Station, industrial areas, and new development. The Repair Shed stood until recently, having been fortified in World War II as a coastal strongpoint.

16 **HARDWICK** [Station 104] It was used by USAAF bombers from December 1942 until June 1945. It had three T2 hangars and a watch office [518/40]. Surviving structures include: one of the communal sites with living huts etc. mainly in tb.

17 **HARLING ROAD** From July 1916 it was a Home Defence squadron base, but expanded between early-1917 and August 1918 to hold three squadrons, being designated No10 Training Depot Station operating until March 1920. It had three double GS hangars, and an Aircraft Repair Shed, as well as the usual workshops, stores and messes. Subsequently it became a storage site for the Army, and, in WWII, a tank repair workshop for US Army. After D-Day, a flying-strip was used by Dakotas carrying out air-drops to the Continent. It now forms Roudham Industrial Estate. Surviving structures include: the ARS of 1917, and many WWII-era huts, workshops, and storage sheds, including rows of Romney huts, in commercial use.

18 **HETHEL** [Station 114] Building commenced in 1941 and the airfield opened late the next year with a succession

100. HETHEL: Gymnasium/chapel now in use as the museum.

of USAAF bomber units. When the Americans left in 1945, the RAF re-established a base but mainly for the disbandment of fighter units. Since 1964 the airfield has provided a home and test-track for Lotus cars. Like Hardwick, the airfield had three T2 hangars and a watch office [type unrecorded]. Surviving structures include: the watch office, three T2 hangars, and the HQ site complete with operations block in the form of a tb hut and Sick quarters; a restored Gymnasium/chapel houses a museum *[100]*, and there is also a further T2 hangar not on its original site, brought in during the 1970s.

19 **HORSHAM ST FAITH** [Norwich] [Station 123] Opened on 1st June 1940, as a base for Blenheims; by early in 1942, Mosquitos were in residence, but only for a while as by the autumn, the USAAF had established a bomber base. After 1945 the RAF returned with fighters until, in 1960, civilian flying took over and continues to this day. Many of the airfield buildings were used in the early days of the University of East Anglia as student accommodation; others are used by local commercial concerns, whilst the rest are part of Norwich Airport. The airfield has five 'C' type hangars and a 'Villa' type watch office [2328-30/39] along with most of the other buildings associated with Expansion Period airfields. The Officers' Mess, once part of UEA's Fifers Lane residential site, has only recently been demolished. Surviving structures include: the five 'C' type-Protected [9181/38] hangars,

101. HORSHAM ST FAITH: Guard-room [494-7'38] reported demolished August 2008.

the 'Villa' watch office, Sickbay / Decontamination Centre; at the very moment of writing , news of the demolition of the Guardhouse [494-7/38] *[101]*, has been received.

20 **LANGHAM** Began life as a satellite of Bircham Newton, sharing many of its parent's activities such as air-sea rescue and army co-operation. By 1944, it had been re-furbished and was operating Beaufighters in an anti-shipping role. In 1947, following

102. LANGHAM: the Dome Trainer, one of only a handful surviving in Britain.

more target-towing and meteorological activities, it became an ELG for Sculthorpe, but was sold in 1961; since then it has been run as a poultry farm by Bernard Matthews. It had three T2 hangars and four Blisters, and a watch office [343/43]. Surviving structures include: the watch office with adjacent fire-tender and fuel-tender sheds; a very rare Dome Trainer for [mainly] AA training *[102]*, one of only a handful left in Britain;

21 **LITTLE SNORING** Opened in July 1943 as a satellite of Foulsham, operating Lancasters. Later, Beaufighters and Mosquitos of bombing support squadrons were based here. Post-WWII units were equipped with Spitfires and Vampires, but closure came in 1958. It had four T2 hangars, two of which were for storing gliders, a single B1, and a watch office [343/43]. Surviving structures include: two T2 hangars, an imported Blister, and the watch office.

22 **LUDHAM** [Station 177] Operated from autumn 1941 as a satellite of Coltishall flying fighters, until late 1945, with a short hiatus during 1944 when plans for USAAF use came to nought. It also operated briefly as a RNAS station, HMS Flycatcher, from August 1944, reverting to RAF use the next year. It had one T2 hangar and four Blisters, and two watch offices. The first was for a fighter satellite airfield [3156/41] with an added switch room [1536/42]. It never received the upper storey added to some of its fellows, as a new watch office was built alongside [343/43]. Surviving structures include: both watch offices, and a Nissen hut used as a fire-tender shed.

23 **MARHAM** This successor to Narborough, opened in April 1937 as a heavy bomber base operating two squadrons of Hendons and Harrows, soon exchanged for Wellingtons. From 1942 until the end of WWII, mainly Mosquitos were based here. An air-strip at Pentney [TF715127] operated 1939-41, as a Relief Landing Ground, since proposed satellites at neither Gooderstone nor Swaffham were built. Following a non-operational period of training on Lancasters and B-29s, the establishment of the V-bomber force saw the arrival of Valiants, Canberras and Victor tankers. A Bloodhound I SAM site was installed in the 1950s. Towards the end of the century there have been Tornados, from 1983 and, more recently, Harriers. The station remains operational. It was built with five 'C' type hangars [1583/35], a 'Fort' type watch office [1959/34], and all the associated

103. MARHAM: the guard-room and missile assembly building of this Bloodhound 1 SAM installation.

buildings of an Expansion Period airfield. In later years many additions and alterations have been made. Refurbishment in the post-War period saw a lengthening of the run-ways, one of 3000 yards and two of 2000 yards, more and thicker concrete hard-standings, and a new control tower [294/45], designed for very heavy bomber stations. More recently new workshops and HAS for the Tornados have been added. Surviving structures include: most of the 1930s buildings, particularly the hangars, the post-War control tower, HAS, the guardroom and missile assembly building *[103]* of the Bloodhound site, and modern workshops.

24 **MATLASKE** [Station 178] A satellite of Coltishall from autumn 1940, using a variety of fighters, until it closed down in 1945. There was an extremely brief occupation during March-April 1944 by 9th USAAF. It had a single B1 hangar and five Blisters. Its first watch office was one designed for a fighter satellite station [18441/41] but this proved inadequate and was replaced with a later model [343/43]. Most of the airfield has been returned to agriculture. Surviving structures include: the odd Nissen hut and not much more.

25 **MATTISHALL** It was a Home Defence base in World War I flying FE-2bs; the

104. NORWICH, Salhouse Road: this factory building, along with another adjacent to it, used by MSI Defence Systems appears to have the characteristic bow-string roof of the GS hangars of Boulton & Paul's Mousehold Heath aerodrome in use in World War I.

airfield was located in the 80 acre [32 hectare] field behind Tollgate Farm on the East Tuddenham road.

26 **METHWOLD** Opened in June 1939 as the satellite of nearby Feltwell. Development was slow, with a regularly manned watch office only appearing in September 1941, and the first T2 hangar a full year later. In Summer 1943 the airfield was shut down for work to be carried out to produce a full-time station adequate for two squadrons, meanwhile taking in No 3 Group Aircrew School. In May 1944 the arrival of an operational Stirling squadron marked the completion of Methwold's conversion into a free-standing station under 3 Group. Following operational duties by Lancaster units, it closed to flying in 1946, having also served as a repatriation point for returning PoWs. There were five T2 hangars, one on the Technical Site and four to the north-east. The watch office model is unrecorded. Glebe House, now demolished, in the woods to the north-east of the airfield, was the centre of the first administrative and communal site. Surviving structures include: two T2 hangars, the Gymnasium/cinema [16428/40 + 8891/42], and some gabled asbestos-sheet huts which may be post-War.

27 **MOUSEHOLD HEATH** [Norwich] had been a training-ground for the Nelson cavalry barracks until taken over by the RFC in 1914. It operated as a training depot until May 1916 when it became a Wing HQ, then an overhaul and repair facility, and then an Aircraft Acceptance Park for aircraft manufactured in Norwich. It had a number of GS hangars and other sheds, prior to

enormous expansion, first as an AAP, then as the Boulton and Paul factory. Surviving structures include: two GS hangars *[104]* and a small Dutch barn-type shed, all on MSI Defence's site on Salhouse Road; other triple gabled sheds etc remain from the Boulton and Paul years up until 1936.

28 **NARBOROUGH** Opened in August 1915, being used by RNAS anti-Zeppelin patrols, but was taken over by the RFC the next year as a Home Defence squadron base, a fighter-training school and a depot. There were six hangars and assorted living huts, messes, workshops etc straddling the road south from Narborough, with a larger, GS hangar, known as the 'red hangar', further west towards the present RAF Marham. It was closed at the end of WWI. Surviving structures include some rebuilt off-site, including the timber village hall at West Acre [TF779151] which was formerly Narborough's officers' mess;

29 **NORTH CREAKE** Beginning life as a decoy field for Docking, from autumn 1943 it provided a home for RAF bomber units displaced by USAAF arrivals, as a sub-station of Foulsham. After a period in Care & Maintenance, it finally closed late in 1947. It had two T2 hangars [3653/42] and one B1, although the 1942 plans show a further two hangar-sites but not that ultimately occupied by the B1. There was a watch office [343/43]. Surviving structures include: the hangars, watch office, now converted to a dwelling, Parachute Store[11137/41] *[105]*, Main Stores and

105. NORTH CREAKE: Parachute Store [10825/42] with Dinghy Store [2901/43]; interestingly, the Air Ministry plan, produced before the airfield was completed, lists a different parachute store design [11137/41], but the parachute store, as built, is the same as Rackheath's [see 107].

Main Workshops in paired Romney huts [5851/42 and 5852/42], Armoury, Maintenance Units, Flight Offices etc in a variety of tb and Nissen hutting, Turret trainer, Bombing teacher, Cinema and stand-by-set houses.

30 **NORTH PICKENHAM** [Station 143] Opened in May 1944 as a USAAF bomber base, operating Liberators, the last of the 8th USAAF's 66 sites, A period of use as a MU followed the end of WWII, then it was chosen as a THOR IRBM site from 1959-63, closing two years later. It had two T2 hangars, and a watch office [343/43]. Surviving structures include: huts and the Operations Block *[106]* with probable Norden bomb-sight Store alongside; all traces of the THOR site have disappeared.

106. NORTH PICKENHAM: Operations Block with, to the side, a secure store for the Norden bomb-sights used by the USAAF.

31 **OLD BUCKENHAM** [Station 144] It was built as a base for USAAF Liberator bombers from late 1943 until mid-'45. It had two T2 hangars and a watch office [343/43]. Surviving structures include: a few huts and later Blister hangars on the site still used for flying.

32 **OULTON** [Street] Opened in July 1940 as a satellite of Horsham St Faith, transferring to Swanton Morley in 1942, and then to Foulsham in 1943, this latter re-organisation entailing a major re-building of accommodation, hangarage and runways in order to operate Fortresses of both RAF and USAAF. For some time, the sixteenth-century Blickling Hall, now a National Trust property, served as a billet for bomber crews. Officers were accommodated in huts in the wooded part of the Park, whilst batmen and clerks slept in the former servants' quarters in the attics. The barns to the east of the Hall's west wing were occupied by the RAF, as were private rooms behind. The Harness-room was the Guard-room, the Officers' mess was in the Hall's east wing, and the Sergeants' Mess was in the present Stewards' room, with the PBX in the basement below the kitchen. From 1945 Oulton was a storage site for the MU at Swannington. It had two T2 hangars. Its original watch office was a Type A for bomber satellites [15898/40] later replaced by the generic 343/43. Surviving structures include: a T2 hangar, Main Stores in Romney huts, and the replacement watch office whose days apparently may be numbered.

33 **PULHAM** This was the Admiralty Airship Experimental Station throughout World War I, after which, it became a storage depot, serving as such until the end of World War II. In 1924, its No.2 Hangar was moved to Cardington [Bedfordshire] where it still stands. Its No.1 Hangar was demolished in 1948. In World War II there was a RDF mast, and an aircraft scrap-yard in the remaining, camouflaged hangar. The rest of the site was run as a SAA and Pyrotechnics store by 53 MU; Surviving structures include: the Silicol Building, some stores, workshops, and living huts; the RNAS officers' mess was in Upper Vaunces Farm.

34 **RACKHEATH** [Station 145] It was in use by Liberators of USAAF from late 1943 until April 1945. It had two T2 hangars and a watch office [343/43]. Surviving structures include: the watch office; a T2 hangar, tb tractor and trailer shed, and Nissen fire-tender shed; Parachute Store [10825/42] *[107]*, and Main Stores in Romney huts.

107. RACKHEATH: Parachute Store [10825/42].

35 SCULTHORPE Was built in 1942, carrying out a range of tasks using, primarily, Mosquitos; in May 1944, it was closed to be converted into a Very Heavy Bomber station, re-opening in February 1949 with USAF B-29s. Fighter-bombers stayed here until 1962, and the station remains as a stand-by airfield. It originally had four T2 hangars, two of which were intended for the storage of gliders, and one B1. It had a watch office for bomber and OTU satellite stations [13726/41]. Its up-grading in 1945 involved extending the runways to one of 3000 yards and two of 2000 yards, building a new control tower [294/45] thereby relegating its predecessor to salt store, and ultimately adapting the hangars as nose-docks. Surviving structures include: the control tower, Blister hangars, nuclear weapons storage and domestic sites.

36 SEDGEFORD Was in use from 1915, with No.3 School of Air Fighting operating from summer 1916 until late the next year when Bircham Newton took over. The airfield lay east of the village and south of the B1454 road at cTF7336. Surviving structures include: the officers' quarters from WWI, and a decoy blockhouse from WWII.

108. SEETHING: Operations Block

37 SEETHING [Station 146] Was used by USAAF Liberators from late-1943 until April 1945. It had two T2 hangars and a watch office for bomber satellites [13726/41]. Surviving structures include: the beautifully-restored watch office, Ops Block *[108]*, and some BCF huts *[109]*.

109. SEETHING: BCF hut.

38 **SHIPDHAM** [Station 115] In use from autumn 1942 until June 1945 as the very first operational USAAF bomber base in Britain. Its main users were Liberator squadrons. Its relatively early construction in the War is reflected in the fact that, like Hardwick, it had three T2 hangars, and also the first of the wartime utility watch office models [518/40 with pre-cast concrete floors, 8936/40]. Surviving structures include: two T2 hangars, the watch office, and assorted tb huts, including that which housed the morgue.

110. SNETTERTON: Bombing Teacher [816/43].

39 **SNETTERTON HEATH** [Station 138] Was occupied by USAAF bombers from mid-1943 until December 1945, latterly flying humanitarian missions. The separate Eccles depot was Station 548. The RAF left in 1949 and the site was sold in 1952, ultimately to be used for motor-racing. It had two T2 hangars and a watch office [343/43]. Surviving structures include: two hangars of the depot, Bombing Teacher [816/43] *[110]*, Fabric Store [12773/41], plus tb and Nissen hutting.

40 **SWANNINGTON** Was used from April 1944 until September 1945 by RAF Mosquito squadrons, the site being finally sold in 1957. It had two T2 hangars, one at each end of the Technical Site, and a single B1, which is shown on the 1944 plan as being on the opposite side of the airfield, but without recording the type. It had a watch office [12779/41]. Haveringland Hall, now ruined, served as the Officers' Mess. Surviving structures include: the watch office, the Fire-tender shed [12410/41 in a Nissen hut], NFE Store [12411/41 in tb] and Floodlight Trailor [sic] and Tractor [also 12411/41].

41 **SWANTON MORLEY** Was begun in early-1939 as a base for Blenheims, with a 'Villa'-type watch office [5845/39], one of the last to be installed, and a 'J' type hangar, the eve-of-war stop-gap design. Later, Bostons and Mitchells were used until Mosquitos became available in numbers. After 1945 a Signals School was in residence for a few years, and the airfield is now the Army's Robertson Barracks, but civilian flying and aircraft construction still take place. It had a mixture of Expansion Period and utility buildings, concentrated technical, administrative and domestic areas, but also four T2 and four Blister hangars dispersed around the airfield. Surviving structures include: the watch office, hangars, and many of the 1930s buildings that only just made it.

42 **THETFORD** [Snarehill Farm] It was set up in autumn 1915 as a training airfield,

becoming No.4 School of Navigation and Bomb-dropping, and closing in 1918. It was re-used as a Bombing Decoy for nearby Honington early in World War II, and in 1942, once the bombing offensive had been largely neutralised, the site became a bombing range for use by both the RAF and USAAF. The airfield had a mixture of GS and Bessonneau hangars with an extensive hutted camp. Surviving structures include: the 367/41 control blockhouse of the decoy, and, beside it, a quadrant tower from the range; near the site of the main gate are the ruins of a double squash court which may be of early design [2078/18] or may date from World War II.

43 **THORPE ABBOTTS** [Station 139] Opened for use by USAAF B-17s in June 1943, and not vacated until December 1945. The RAF relinquished the airfield in 1956. It now serves as an aviation museum, and for agriculture. It had two T2 hangars and a watch office designed for bomber satellites [13726/41] with the Seco additional observation cabin [[5966/43] anchored to the roof. Surviving structures include: the watch office, NFE Store, and several Nissen huts, all perfectly restored.

44 **TIBENHAM** [Station 124] It was used by USAAF Liberators from November 1943 until June 1945. The airfield closed in 1959 but is still used for gliding. It had two T2 hangars. Its original Type B bomber satellite watch office was subsequently enhanced with the customary first-floor observation room [13079/41]. Little remains beyond a few huts.

45 **WATTON** [Station 376] Opened in early-1939 for use by Blenheims until January 1942, when an Advanced Flying training unit was formed to acclimatise pilots trained abroad to the conditions of the Europe. In mid-1943 the USAAF moved in with a maintenance depot for Liberators [Neaton depot, Station 505] and meteorological and reconnaissance units flying B-17s, B-24s and Mosquitos. In September 1945, the return of the RAF brought the Radio Warfare and the Central Signals Establishments, and a Bloodhound I SAM squadron was based here in the 1950s. RAF activities ceased around 1997. It had most of the buildings expected on an Expansion Period airfield built through the 1930s, including four 'C' type hangars [2029/34, 3264/35 etc], a 'Fort'-type watch office [207/36], officers' and sergeants' messes, stores and workshops etc. A new watch office was supplied [12779/41 or 343/43] and this has served the station ever since with the addition of a VCR. Two B1 three T2 and Robin hangars have also been added; also a massive concrete Uniter communications building, resembling a 1980s War Operations Centre. Surviving structures include: most of the 1930s buildings as well as the later ones, and, next to the living site with its H-blocks and Institute, a Gymnasium/chapel, now a nursery.

NB: during 2008 many of those structures on the airfield [south of the B1108], including all the 'C'type hangars, were demolished.

111. WEST RAYNHAM: Air Defence Tactical Training Theatre [ADT3] used for training on the Rapier missile [cf 102].

46 **WENDLING** [Station 118] It was built in 1942 for use by USAAF Liberators, flying over 7000 missions by April 1945. It was a stand-by airfield until vacated by the RAF in 1961, since when it has reverted to agriculture and poultry farming. It had two T2 hangars, and a watch office of apparently unique design, according to the official plan [5852/41 and 1200/43]. Surviving structures include: tb and Nissen huts on communal sites, some containing wall-art are in commercial use.

47 **WEST RAYNHAM** Opened in 1939 for use by Blenheims, and a variety of target-towing aircraft, but by the end of 1943 it was part of the Bomber Support Group operating Mosquitos. After 1945 it was home to the Central Fighter Establishment and other development units, but in 1960 it was again operational with Javelins, then Canberras, and finally Hunters. Flying terminated in1975. Throughout the 1960s, 1970s and into the 1980s, a protective screen was extended over East Anglia by the Bloodhound II SAMs based here, with their central servicing facilities. It was built as a classic Expansion Period airfield with four 'C' type hangars and a 'Fort'-type watch office [207/36] but later modified with a new upper storey. Post-War up-grading gave it expanded hard-standing and a new control tower [294/45] with adjacent fire-

112. OLD CATTON: original building from RAF Old Catton, now HQ Norfolk ATC, but once one of Coltishall's dispersed Operations Centres.

station. The Bloodhound installations and the maintenance centre are on the opposite side of the airfield from the main site.A Rapier Dome Trainer, or ADT3 *[111]*, stands near the hangar arc. Surviving structures include: most of the 1930s airfield, both watch offices, the Dome Trainer, and the church. In late-2007, many of the remaining married-quarters were sold off to private buyers.

48 **WEYBOURNE** This airstrip was established in the mid-1930s for aircraft which towed targets for the AA practice camp. After 1942, catapult-launched targets had taken over and, after the War, pilot-less aircraft were used until the site closed in 1958.

Airfield-related buildings

Depots [RAF Maintenance Units etc] are listed in Chapter 5, but it is relevant to note here the existence of two alternative off-site Operations Rooms for RAF Coltishall at RAF Old Catton *[112]*, the timber building now occupied by the Norfolk ATC HQ, and also Stratton Strawless Hall, just off the A140 Norwich-Aylsham road.

DEFENCE AGAINST AIR ATTACK 4

Air defence in World War I

On the evening of 19th January 1915, three German naval airships set off across the North Sea to bomb the industrial areas of the Humber estuary. Two of them made it to the Norfolk coast using the Happisburgh lightship, anchored eight miles [13km] out to sea, as a marker. One then turned south and dropped nine bombs on Great Yarmouth, whilst the other bombed Kings Lynn, killing two and injuring 13, the first casualties of aerial bombardment of the war. As an immediate response to this and several subsequent random attacks on East Anglia, a mobile force with Vickers machine-guns and searchlights mounted on lorries, was assembled at Newmarket, to be alerted by telephone by any police or military personnel spotting a Zeppelin. This was more in the way of a public relations exercise than a military solution, but it pointed the way to future developments. Although London was usually the intended target for the majority of the Zeppelin raids, the route taken was always over the Norfolk coast, so the decision was taken to locate a significant portion of the AA defences there to intercept the raiders before they could do too much damage. A detachment of two 3 pounder guns, some Rolls-Royce armoured cars with machine-guns, and a searchlight had spent the summer at North Walsham, and now, in August 1916, the RNAS Mobile AA Brigade, presently based in London, set up at Bacton with its HQ in Grammar School Road, North Walsham. It comprised 12 of the newly-acquired French 75mm Auto-cannons mounted on Panhard or de Dion Bouton tourers with strengthened chassis, and three searchlights on trucks. Two of these guns and one of the searchlights were soon detached to protect Sandringham House, where Queen Alexandra was often in residence, the crews being billeted in the school-house. The intention was to work with the RNAS fighters based at Bacton and Holt, but the major problem was predicting the direction from which the airship would appear, especially under cloudy conditions. Experiments were conducted using stethoscopes attached to megaphones, actually gramophone trumpets, linked up to directional pointers with compass cards. So as the listener heard the magnified sound of the Zeppelin engines through the stethoscope, he would turn his head in the direction of its approach, thus indicating a bearing which might inform the gun-layers on the ground, and the pilots about to take off. Another technique involved keeping coops full of pheasants at Winterton. These birds had extremely sensitive hearing and reacted audibly to the sound of approaching aircraft-engines long before human ears could pick it up, but they gave little reliable

113. HUNSTANTON: the lighthouse was used by the Y Service in World War I, and after the top storey had been rebuilt in 1939, by the Royal Observer Corps in World War II.

indication of direction. Dedicated listening-posts, manned mainly by coastguards, sometimes amateur radio-hams, and RNVR personnel, were set up by Lt Cdr Hippisley, in Hunstanton. These posts were equipped with radio-receivers so that they could listen in to German radio traffic generally, but especially to that between airships and their bases. Aerials were mounted on the lighthouse *[113]* for this purpose; there was a second post in Downs Road, and a third in Cromer Road, with the old wooden Golf Club-house being taken over. Having already cracked the German navigation codes it was often possible to pinpoint specific aircraft through triangulation, by locking on to German broadcasts with more than one receiver. There was a network of Royal Naval Wireless Stations linked to Room 40 at the Admiralty, and these contributed to the operations of the 'Y Service', the listeners and interceptors. There were also a smaller number of stations which comprised the 'Z Service', whose function is not clear now, although they were possibly credited with being able to carry out radio-direction-finding. Hunstanton was coded as a 'Y/Z Station'.

Meanwhile, the Mobile Brigade at Bacton continued trying to shoot down Zeppelins with little discernible success. Although no permanent buildings appear to have been constructed for their AA guns, at least one double gun-pit was constructed with sandbags for its superstructure, but with a dug-out for shelter from the cruel east wind. A turntable mounting had been developed giving the guns 360 degrees of traverse, and these were incorporated into this emplacement, along with the height-finding, range-finding and aiming instruments. After Christmas 1917, the RNAS guns were moved south into Essex to defend London against the new threat posed by the Gotha heavy bombers, but their place was taken by Army batteries with 13 pounder guns, Nos. 1, 2 and 3 AA Mobile Batteries being based at Eaton Hall, Norwich. Apart from these RNAS and Army mobile brigades, Norfolk had never had many fixed AA guns. The aerodrome at Great Yarmouth had two AA guns; the airship experimental station at Pulham had three 3 inch [75mm] guns and three searchlights; and two of the night landing-grounds, Bacton and Holt, each had an AA gun and a searchlight. By 1917, all the East Anglian AA defences were administered from Harwich, but still included several sites in Norfolk including Pulham, which now had one 3 inch [75mm] gun, located at The Beeches, just to the east of the airship station; and three sites in Great Yarmouth, including one at Nelson's Monument, each equipped with an 18 pounder AA gun. This was probably the adaptation of that gun which allowed a re-lined 18 pounder barrel to fire a 13 pound shell with an 18 pound cartridge.

Air defence between the wars

Although there was an effective, integrated air defence system in place in 1918, with guns, searchlights, fighters, observers and listeners, all working together efficiently, the end of World War I, nevertheless, saw an almost complete dismantling of these AA defences. A succession of national air defence plans in the 1920s and early-1930s were all based on the London Air Defence Area [LADA] which covered little more than the capital. With the exception of Harwich, continuing as a naval base, East Anglia remained defenceless against aerial attack. It was only in 1935, with the Re-Orientation Plan's acceptance of a threat from Germany, that defences began to face east across the North Sea. An extension of the existing plans placed an Outer Artillery Zone up the line of the A1 road, with an Aircraft Fighting Zone immediately to its west. At this time, acoustics still appeared to provide the means of detecting incoming aircraft, and Radar, or Radio Direction Finding [RDF] was still a little way off, as was a replacement for

114. NORWICH: the TA Centre in Aylsham Road which was built as the base for the newly-formed 78th HAA Regiment in 1939.

the 3 inch [75mm] 20 cwt [995kg] HAA gun. In 1935, the responsibility for defending the country against aerial bombardment was handed to the Territorial Army. It would be the volunteers who would use the new 3.7 inch HAA guns and their accompanying searchlights, predictors and range-finders. Around this time, the 84th [East Anglian] Field Brigade RA [TA] moved out of their drill hall in the Georgian Ivory House on All Saints' Green, in Norwich, for their new purpose-built premises in Aylsham Road *[114]*, opened in 1939. They had been reorganised as 78th [1st East Anglian] Anti-Aircraft Brigade RA [TA] in 1938. Training took place in the new drill hall and at out-lying detachments around the county. The architect, Cecil Upcher also produced plans for accompanying RASC and RAOC units, but these were never realised. Much of the brand-new AA equipment was held in Mobilisation Centres, run by a cadre of regular artillery-men, artificers, armourers and store-men. Such buildings survive at Setchey, near Kings Lynn, at Fakenham, and at Arminghall *[115]*, south of Norwich, now the Syfer factory.

Air defence in World War II

The outbreak of war in September 1939 saw some parts of the system better-prepared than others. Many of RDF's operating problems had been solved, and the basic Chain Home [CH] network extended around the east coast from Dover to Yorkshire, with Air Ministry Experimental Stations [AMES] at West Beckham and Stoke Holy Cross. Bircham Newton was home to the Blenheims of 235 Squadron, belonging to No 16 Group, Coastal Command. The fighters, Hurricanes of 242 Squadron, and Spitfires

115. ARMINGHALL: The Mobilisation Centre established as a store for the TA's AA equipment in the period leading up to the outbreak of World War II, and then as a maintenance and supply base for AA guns throughout the war.

of 66 Squadron were based in the Sector Station of Coltishall, with satellites at Ludham and Matlaske, reporting to 12 Group, Fighter Command, based at Watnall near Nottingham, but being directed from an Operations Room on the Sector Airfield at Duxford, near Cambridge. Decisions were influenced by information gleaned from two sources. Firstly from radio-intercepts by the Y-Service, whose Plot-rooms were at Trimingham and Winterton, and later on at Sheringham as well, and secondly by sightings of aircraft, relayed by the [Royal] Observer Corps with its web of observation posts, supplemented by Coastguard stations and free-lance observers. The ROC in Norfolk was co-ordinated by No 16 Group HQ in Norwich. Guns and searchlights were very thin on the ground. Neither the 1936 plan nor its 1939 revision had allowed for any HAA guns or searchlights at all in Norfolk, but some were indeed allocated to Norwich and to some of the airfields, with some LAA weapons sent to protect Stoke Holy Cross and Denver Sluice. Watlington Hall near Downham Market became the HQ of 64 Searchlight Regiment whose scattered sites covered a wide area. Most of the established airfields had bombing decoy sites, Bircham Newton, for instance, is fairly typical in having three such sites by mid-1940 at the latest. The fear of aerial bombardment of civilian targets prompted the building of air-raid shelters, the use of barrage balloons, and other such passive air defence measures. Prior to the general introduction of VHF radio for communication between fighters and their controllers, radio DF stations were established at Stowupland [Suffolk] and Barton Bendish [Norfolk] to increase the range of 12 Group fighter control at Duxford. Similar DF stations were set up at Shropham [Norfolk] and Wix [Essex] to improve 11 Group control at Debden.

AA artillery in World War II

Guns, especially HAA guns were in short

supply throughout the war. Norfolk's AA defences were controlled by 41 AA Brigade which shared HQ with Sector J fighters at RAF Coltishall, and by 40 AA Brigade based first at Duxford, and then at nearby Pampisford Hall [Cambridgeshire]. However scarce the guns were, it was still vital to protect certain targets. The only HAA guns available were manned by 78 HAA Regt, and Marham, Feltwell and Watton each had four old 3 inch guns to defend them. The remaining battery stayed in Norwich, on two sites named X and Y. The 40mm Bofors LAA gun was in even shorter supply so priority went to protecting the air defence infra-structure itself. Coltishall had four guns manned by 36 Mobile LAA Regiment, and the RDF stations at West Beckham and Stoke Holy Cross had three each, supplemented by 8 Lewis LAA lmgs. This meant that everywhere else had only LAA lmgs to defend them, provided by 29 LAA Regiment whose HQ were at Kipton House, Weasenham moving, by January 1941, to Swardeston House in Norwich. Its personnel manned Lewis LAA lmgs at West Raynham [8], Marham [16], Bircham Newton [8], Denver Sluice [12] plus those at the RDF sites, and the other airfields. Its batteries were thus dispersed across Norfolk, 108 Battery, for instance, being based at Leicester Square Farm, South Creake. Similarly, the searchlights of 41 Brigade, were scattered around with 60 Regiment at Croxton Park, Thetford, 64 Regiment at Watlington Hall near Downham Market, 65 Regiment at Aylsham Manor House, and 69 Regiment at Redcliffe Hall, Brundall. Individual searchlight batteries were deployed across the area, 64 Regiment's 441 Bty. being based at Beaupre Hall, Outwell for instance. Many of those manning searchlight sites had been drafted in from other units, as had many pre-War TA infantry units which were converted to AA troops. Thus 444 Bty. of the 65 Searchlight Regiment based at Wolterton Park had been a company of the 2/6 Bn. Essex Regiment. The batteries of 69 S/L Regiment, numbered 206-214, were at Thetford, East Harling [Beacon Hill Camp], Cavick [Wymondham], Raveningham [Orchards], Brundall, Aylsham, Guist, South Raynham and Narborough, some of these sites having previously been occupied by 60 and 65 Regiments. A regime of continuous experimentation prevailed necessitating the constant re-siting of lights in belts and clusters, involving the use of dozens of different locations. Whilst the early sites may still often be identified by the presence of a pillbox, countless subsequent ones are now little more than map-references. Throughout 1941, a number of new developments took place, most notably the use of Gunlaying [GL] Radar which helped the guns to pick up targets more easily. The Norwich site had a set early in 1941, but it was taken away and sent to Merseyside whose need, presumably, was greater. In April 1942, Norwich was subjected to one of the retaliatory Baedeker raids. As a response, eight 3.7 inch mobile HAA guns of 106 HAA Regiment arrived from the Great Yarmouth/Lowestoft Gun-defended Area [GDA] to set up a new Norwich GDA.

116. GORLESTON: 221 Beccles Road, once the 'Cavalier' PH and now a Veterinary Practice, but during World War II, the Gun Operations Room for the Yarmouth/Lowestoft Gun-Defended Area.

Three sites were established, the existing 3 inch one at RAF Horsham St Faith [NH1], and two new ones for the 3.7 inch guns on Mousehold Heath [NH2] and at Broomhill, Church Lane, Eaton [NH3]. In addition, a new unit was formed with HQ in Unthank Road, to man 3 inch Un-rotated Rocket Projectile Launchers, known as Z Batteries, with twin projectors on each of the three sites. One 9-barrel launcher was soon added to each of NH2 and NH3. By June 1942, however, the four old 3 inch guns had been sent to Great Yarmouth. Great Yarmouth had five HAA sites with a further three in Lowestoft making up the GDA. In June 1942, three of Great Yarmouth's sites were armed, West Caister [YH1] and Gorleston [YH3] each having four 3.7 inch guns and Mark II GL radar, whilst Race Course [YH4] had the four 3 inch guns from Norwich. All were manned by 106 HAA Regiment with its HQ at 221 Beccles Road, Gorleston *[116]*, also the GDA's Operations Room. By this time all the old 3 inch guns had been removed from the airfields they had protected in 1940. In their place, each airfield had a troop of four Bofors 40mm LAA guns, now manned by the RAF Regiment, plus assorted Quadruple Vickers machine-guns, 20mm Oerlikon or Hispano-Suiza guns, aircraft cannon, or Brens on LAA mountings. Unit diaries show that guns, crews and equipment were being moved around constantly, and there was a continuous movement of 20mm and 40mm guns in and out of the AA Ordnance Depot at Arminghall.

Just when things might have been thought to have settled down, there came a fresh aerial onslaught. In June 1944 the first V1 flying-bomb landed in south-east England. From then until September, thousands of ground-launched V1s arrived causing enormous numbers of casualties and damage. From mid-September, these missiles were launched from aircraft, and whilst a high percentage was destroyed by AA guns and aircraft, it was feared that the target area would now widen. Consequently, the belt of AA guns was extended. The anti-V1 operation was known as Diver so the guns were deployed in the Diver-Box around the Thames Estuary, and the first extension along the coast of East Anglia, became the Diver-Strip, reaching as far as the Cockle Lightship in the Yarmouth GDA opposite Hemsby. Fortunately for the local inhabitants only 13 flying-bombs out of the 10 000 launched hit targets in Norfolk. However the long-range rockets, or V2s, 1400 of which were launched between September 1944 and March 1945, were targeted specifically at Norwich and Ipswich for a period of three weeks between September and October 1944, with 29 landing in Norfolk. There was no realistic counter to these rockets once they were launched as it was calculated that if one were picked up on the radar and 400 HAA shells were fired at it, there would be a one in thirty chance of hitting it. However, the descent of so much AA shrapnel would have caused more damage than the rockets themselves, many of which fell in open countryside. The Diver-Strip AA sites were quite substantial, with four gun-pits, each with a platform of railway-sleepers bearing the holdfast for the electrically-operated 3.7 inch HAA gun, laid by GL radar on its circular mat, with the tracking equipment on a scaffolding platform alongside. Living quarters, offices, crew-shelters, workshops and magazines all were to the rear. Only the two northern-most sites of the Fringe lay in Norfolk. One lay between the coast road and Gorleston Cliffs, opposite where now the hospital stands, identified as YH2 in 1942 but not previously armed. The other one was the established YH1 West Caister site, just over half a mile [1km] due south of Caister Hall. Each had four 3.7 inch HAA guns and both sites were crewed by 139 [Mixed] HAA Regiment, so most of the instruments were operated by women of the ATS, who will have carried out many of the other battery duties as well. The Strip extended five miles [8km] out to sea, and half that distance inland. Fighter Command was warned that as AA guns would be engaging any visible targets in that area, their pilots should keep clear. Towards the end of the V1 season, the guns were achieving an 82% success rate in shooting them down. The only way of countering V2s, however, was by stopping them at source by bombing either the launch-sites, or the supply-routes by which fuel and the rockets themselves were delivered.

Bombing decoys

One alternative strategy to defend against aerial bombardment was to confuse the incoming bombers by providing spurious targets. This was achieved by building shadow sites, some distance away from the genuine targets, but close enough to be credible. These decoys took two different forms. The K-site was for daylight use and involved the construction of a dummy airfield with mock-up aircraft, often made by scenery studios in the film industry. Fake aircraft on decoys for Norfolk airfields included Wellingtons at Feltwell, Marham and Swanton Morley, and Blenheims at Bircham Newton and Foulsham. These would be moved around to simulate an active operation. A small ground-crew of twenty or so RAF personnel remained on site to maintain this deception, and was thoughtfully provided with a splinter-proof shelter. Eye-witness accounts suggest that some of these dummy wooden aircraft may have been manufactured at the Boulton & Paul works on Salhouse Road, Norwich. The Q-site was for night-time use and relied on timing. At the sound of approaching aircraft, lights simulating a flare-path, and a Chance-light, swung slowly through ninety degrees to simulate the ground lighting used on an actual airfield, would be extinguished just after the hostile aircraft could be expected to have spotted them. Decoy flare-paths changed as the real ones evolved, from T-type to Drem to Avenue and so on. All these lights were operated electrically from a semi-sunken control bunker, containing generators, and manned by a permanent crew of two. The Chance-light was mounted on a bracket on top of the bunker itself. A simple night-shelter design [3395/40] appears early on, superseded by a more complex design [367/41] as the lighting techniques improved. The basic idea of decoys had appeared towards the end of World War I, in France, and was developed now by Colonel Turner's Department at the Air Ministry which co-ordinated a programme nationally. Colonel Turner had previously been Director of Works and Buildings and had an unrivalled knowledge of airfield layouts. Operating into 1941, K-sites were deemed ineffective for many reasons, and many closed. Whilst the Luftwaffe had recognised many of the daylight sites as dummies, the Q-sites generally escaped detection as fakes, and 80% of them were bombed, often to a greater extent than the genuine airfields they were protecting. A further type of decoy was the QF-site which consisted of fires, in troughs and braziers, often oil-based, intended to simulate burning incendiaries. Intermittently, flares were built into the sequence for added realism. These were initially for use on airfields but were developed as Starfish-sites for the protection of cities, naval bases, munitions factories and troop concentrations. One of Norwich's Starfish-sites, managed to attract almost half the bombs intended for the city, during one of the Baedeker raids of May 1942. It would appear that a stray bomb had actually ignited a flare, which then acted as a magnet to many of the bomber aircraft, a sort of self-service decoy. Added to the ARP authorities' relief was the fact that despite such large numbers of bombs being dropped nearby, Stoke Holy Cross radar site somehow avoided taking hits. Some very sophisticated QL-sites were also constructed to mimic specific situations such as marshalling-yards or dock lights. Flickering lights were used to simulate ineffective black-out, and the crew at one Norfolk decoy site found that simply placing a light-fitting, with an illuminated bulb, inside a box with the lid propped half-open, could give the impression from the air, of a lighted room with the window left open. All these types of decoy were provided with control bunkers for the crew, with a specialist design [CT 151/41] for QL-sites. In the run-up to the D-Day landings, Operation Fortitude was a deception exercise, promoting the notion of an invasion of the Pas de Calais involving a build-up of forces in East Anglia. A number of sites around the Norfolk Broads were included in these deception activities.

There were examples of most of these types of decoy site in Norfolk. There were K-sites

117. THETFORD, Snarehill: used as an airfield in World War I, this area was a decoy airfield and then a bombing range in World War II; this picture shows the control blockhouse of the bombing decoy [TL901814].the newly-formed 78th HAA Regiment in 1939.

at Bircham Newton, West Raynham, Marham, Swanton Morley, Foulsham and Feltwell, all of whom had several Q-sites as well, along with others including Horsham St Faith, Watton, Langham and Bodney. Some later made use of existing Q-sites, as when Downham Market shared South Acre and Wormegay with Marham, or Langham shared Salthouse and Burnham Sutton with Bircham Newton. Owing both to the secrecy surrounding these installations, and to their ephemeral nature, there are a number of discrepancies between the documentary evidence, anecdotal reporting, and the results of fieldwork. Barton Bendish, Bodney and Docking have all been claimed as decoys, but do not show up in the documents. Coxford Heath, one of Bircham Newton's original Q/K-sites, ended up perilously close to Sculthorpe, but is listed as that airfield's own Q-site. Docking's own Q-site at North Creake was right on the edge of the new airfield. In addition to the airfield decoys, there were "N" series naval decoys at Somerton/Winterton Ness and Lound protecting the Great Yarmouth naval base. The Somerton site started life as a hybrid K/Q-site with railway track laid so that a dummy aircraft could be propelled along it, and lit to simulate an aircraft landing.

Civil decoys were built at Little Plumstead, Bramerton and Horning to protect Norwich at the time of the Baedeker raids. Little Plumstead and Bramerton continued in use as permanent Starfish-sites and were then further developed as QL-sites, Little Plumstead simulating the marshalling yards and factory lighting of Boulton and Paul's engineering works, and Bramerton seeking to mimic the locomotive glows of Norwich's main railway marshalling yards. Horning is also reported in use specifically as a railway decoy but does not appear in the documents. It may have been added into the scheme on local initiative. A number of the control bunkers can still be seen at, for instance, Wormegay, South Acre, Thetford [Snarehill] *[117]*, and Sedgeford.

Other AA measures

Amongst the ingenious devices developed for the protection of airfields was the Parachute and Cable [PAC]. This consisted of a salvo of eight or nine rockets which were fired into the air trailing steel cables. At a height of around 600 feet [180m] a parachute opened, tautening the suspended cable. If an aircraft hit it, a second parachute opened forcing the trapped aircraft to tow the encumbered cable behind it, slowing it down and rendering it more vulnerable to ground-fire.

On a much larger scale were Barrage-balloons, tethered at 5000 feet [1500m] by a steel cable. If an aircraft hit the cable it was designed to break at top and bottom, and parachutes opened to create sufficient drag to bring the aircraft down as it lugged all this behind it. The aerial trials of these techniques, sponsored by the Royal Aircraft Establishment [Farnborough], were completed over Norfolk, when an intrepid RAF pilot actually flew a variety of aircraft into cables varying in thickness and suspended from both parachutes and balloons. From April 1942, Norwich was protected by balloons flown from 19 sites around the city, mainly school-playgrounds, sports fields, and waste-, common- or pasture-land. The balloons were handled by RAF and WRAF personnel. During the Baedeker raids of 1942, at least one enemy aircraft was thought to have been brought down by the barrage, but its general benefit was in forcing the bombers to stay above 8000 feet [2450m] to be safe, thus spreading the bombs over a wider area, and thus causing less damage than if they had all fallen on the small, tightly-packed nucleus of the city.

An offensive use of balloon technology was developed by the Boom Defence Department at Landguard Fort [Suffolk]. Small hydrogen gas-filled balloons carrying incendiary devices or small bombs were released to drift over the North Sea with the intention of creating havoc amongst, primarily, the enemy's power-lines. Around half of the balloons trailed 300 foot [90m] long steel cables. Nearly 100 000 balloons were released between March 1942 and June 1944 causing enormous damage to crops, power supply, woodland, and food stocks across Europe, as far afield as Italy

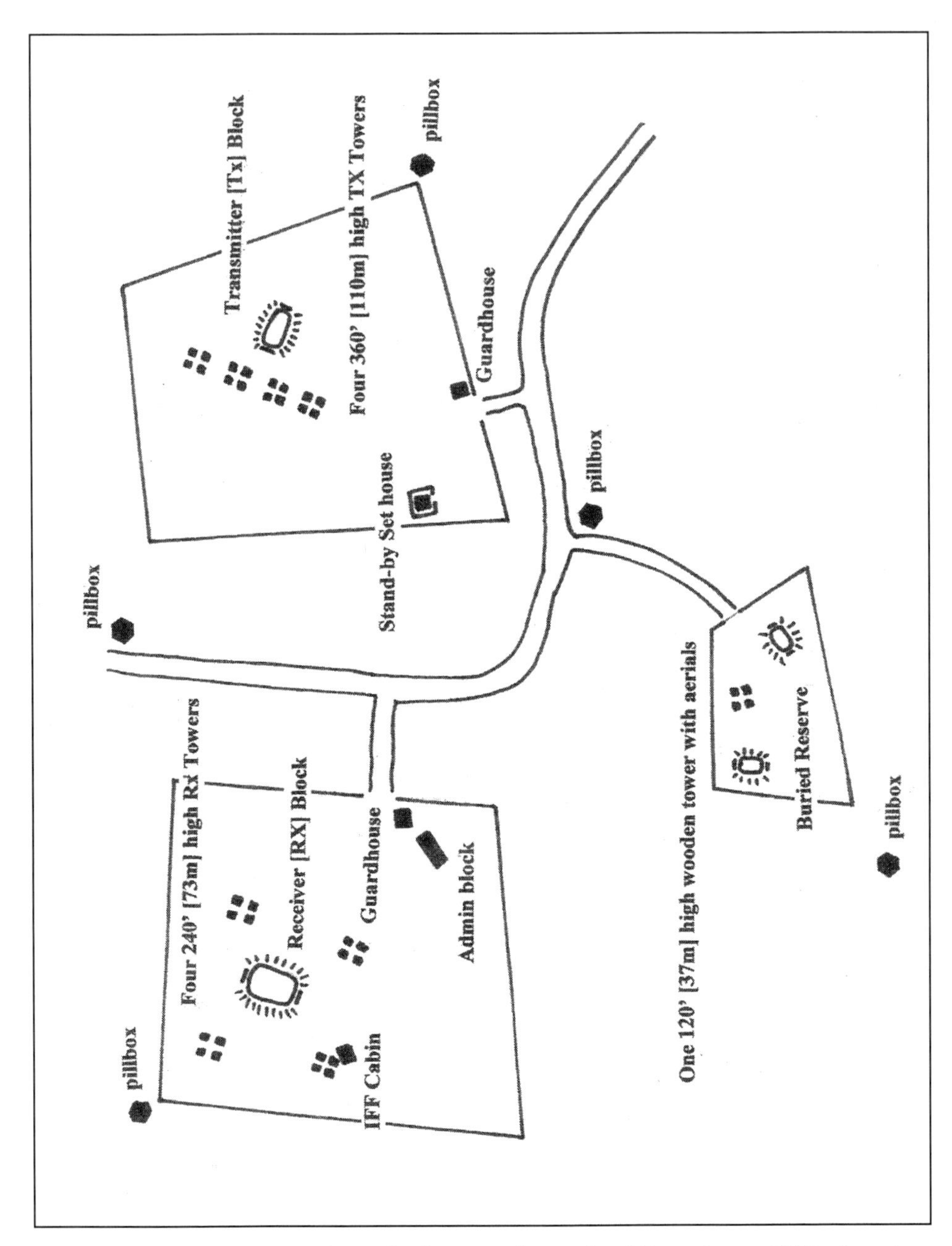

Figure 15 Sketch plan to show the layout of standard East Coast CH Radar sites such as Stoke Holy Cross and West Beckham

118. STOKE HOLY CROSS: the survivor from the four Transmitter Towers which once stood at this Chain Home radar site.

119. STOKE HOLY CROSS: the Transmitter block of the Chain Home radar site.

and Bulgaria. In 1943, an additional Outward site was opened at Waxham operated, as was its parent site, by WRNS personnel.

Radar in World War II

Although experiments with acoustic devices for detecting approaching aircraft ceased in Norfolk at the end of World War I, East Anglia was central to the development of Radio Direction-finding, or Radar. Alongside the better-known experimental work at Bawdsey and Orfordness [both in Suffolk], some similar experimental work was also carried out at the Pulham airship station.

By 1940, the basic Chain Home RDF system was in place with radar sites, or Air Ministry Experimental Stations [AMES] as they were still then known, established at West Beckham and Stoke Holy Cross, two of the original 15 sites planned in 1937 *[Figure 15]*. These sites had four 240 foot-high [73m] wooden Receiver Towers grouped in a square around the brick-built Receiver [Rx] Block. Close by was the line of four 350 foot-high [107m] steel Transmitter Towers *[118]* with their Transmitter [Tx] Block *[119]* alongside. Buildings such as these blocks and the generator houses were protected by earth traverses, there was a Buried Reserve [Rx and Tx] for emergency use, and the whole site was surrounded by dacoit fencing with distinctive guardhouse at the entrance *[120]*, and pillboxes around the perimeter. Within a short time a Chain Home Low [CHL] station, for detecting aircraft approaching below 500 feet [150m], was added to the chain at Happisburgh, one of the first to open and linked to Stoke Holy Cross. These were equipped with aerials on either low platforms, or 185 foot [56m] high

120. WEST BECKHAM: the Guard-house of the Chain Home radar site.

towers depending on their height above sea-level, as local conditions influenced the working of the equipment to a far greater extent than in CH stations. Usually the gantries carrying the rotating aerials straddled the timber or brick Rx and Tx huts, 30-60 yards apart. A guard hut, standby-set house and shelters completed the layout of the CHL site. The next big development in radar was the network of Ground-Controlled Interception [GCI] radar stations built to enable fighters more effectively to engage enemy aircraft by being directed onto their specific and individual targets from the ground. Coltishall was to be served by the new GCI station at Neatishead, which opened in autumn 1941, but from July, Happisburgh, with intermediate equipment, had been filling in, both using Mobile GCI equipment. A series of refinements to the GCI programme culminated in the Final GCI design, which employed a frame, 30 x 25 feet [9 x 7.5m] and 5 feet [1.5m] deep, to which were fitted three aerials, the whole rotating on a column. The operations block, known as the Happidrome, was a two-level, brick-built structure, in which the Controller in his elevated cabin, could scan the table on which information was constantly being up-dated. A fully-equipped example may be seen at Neatishead, where it remained in service until 1993.

It had been the army who had originally developed the CHL system for coast defence purposes, but in 1941 it was decided that separate systems for aircraft and ship identification would be wasteful. Therefore the next development of CD/CHL radar would be joint, and 120 sites were chosen, including Winterton, Hopton, Hunstanton, Trimingham, Bard Hill and the already-operating Happisburgh. Both Hopton and Happisburgh used the 185 foot [56m] high tower. West Beckham had CHL equipment mounted on one of its CH transmitter towers in 1942, and the new improved Type 55 radar in 1945. The development of centimetric radar brought about another re-organisation, with the new equipment being installed at Trimingham and Hopton in late-1942. Hunstanton was declared redundant by the end of 1942, as was Winterton by the end of 1943. Attempts had been made to jam Britain's CH system, and J Watch was set up to monitor this, using mobile equipment, located close to operational CH stations. The Avenue, near Stoke Holy Cross, was selected as one such location. Similarly, there were schemes to jam the German bombers' navigational beams, and these involved West Beckham, equipped with a Hallicrafters receiver for

121. BARD HILL: one aerial base and the Identification Friend or Foe [IFF] hut of the radar station.

monitoring of Knickerbein and other, parallel activities at Drayton. Scole was home to a Meacon jamming operation. The CD/CHL station at Trimingham, acted as a Cat station using Type 9000 radar, as part of the British navigational beam operation known as Gee, with a fake cover known as J, and a later refinement to facilitate blind bombing, called Oboe. This function was duplicated nearby at Winterton, and their companion Mouse station was at Walmer [Kent]. Another aspect of RDF was the Identifier Friend or Foe [IFF] system which enabled incoming aircraft to be identified. This equipment was housed in a small brick hut, with examples of such structures surviving at Stoke Holy Cross and at Bard Hill *[121]*.

Norfolk is fortunate to retain the remains of several radar sites. Stoke Holy Cross is a fairly typical east coast CH site. One rectangular area, enclosed by a fence contains the Transmitter block, and one of the four steel Transmitter towers, albeit minus the cantilevered platforms, but, nevertheless, a very rare survival, one of only half-a-dozen or so nationally. In that same enclosure is a 1960s Microwave tower. A second enclosure, again surrounded by a fence, and entered past the standard guard-room, contains the Receiver block, the IFF cabin, and the four squares, each of four concrete plinths which supported the four Receiver towers. A workshop, dating from c1946 is now a residence, and the site is beautifully maintained. Many of these same elements may also be seen at West Beckham, a similar site. Neatishead, whilst presenting itself as a largely Cold War site, retains the 1942 Happidrome still kitted out as a control centre, and forming the basis of the national Radar Museum and Archive, which opens to the public on a regular basis, despite being entirely run by volunteers.

The Royal Observer Corps in Norfolk in World War II

One of the positive things discovered from London's air defence plan in World War I, was the value of a comprehensive network of aircraft-spotters, able to communicate quickly with the AA defences, and with fighter-control. Consequently, the general expansion of the armed forces of the early-1930s included widening the Observer Corps ['Royal' from 1941] network from the Home Counties to most of England. Number 16 Group, based in Norwich, and reporting to Uxbridge, had been proposed in 1924, but was just coming together ten years later. This essentially civilian organisation, composed of volunteers was to become a well-trained and highly-skilled force, complementing the more highly technical contributions of radar and the Y-Service. The Coastguard service was also expanded as war approached, to carry out general coast-watching tasks. Observer Corps posts, often resembling garden-sheds, were established with rudimentary sighting and plotting equipment, and, most necessary of all, telephones. An improvement, the Mickelthwait Height Correction Attachment was issued to posts from August 1940. This very basic equipment was to last into the 1950s. Norwich's ROC Centre was hit hard during the Baedeker raids of June, 1942, when the main telephone cable was severed, cutting off all but two posts from Group HQ, which had to decamp to its emergency centre. Some posts, Brundall, Docking and Melton Constable for instance, were equipped with GL radar in order to carry out Friend or Foe [IFF] interrogation of aircraft. Others, code-named Darky, such as Loddon were provided with high frequency radio-sets in order to help lost or distressed aircraft. As GCI radar came on stream in 1943, the ROC became part of a more integrated system, 16 Group at Norwich, working with RAF Coltishall, and Neatishead GCI Station. The ROC Group HQ was, initially from 1934, in the basement of the GPO's premises in Dove Street, Norwich. Office staff vacancies were filled by Norwich Union Insurance personnel. In 1940 it moved to the new GPO site in St Andrews, then in 1942, to Fairfield in Lime Tree Road, although St Andrews was retained, and indeed used, as an emergency centre. At the outbreak of war, 16 Group consisted of 47 posts scattered across the county, usually working together in threes and fours.

Civil defence

Early in the war, Norwich City Council examined a scheme to excavate air-raid shelters in the city's underlying chalk, under the Castle for example. It would have cost £2.5m for 170,000 places, and was way beyond the council's budget, so the citizens of Norwich had to make do with brick-built communal surface shelters, family Anderson shelters, and indoor Morrison shelters. One of the brick-built shelters for 50 persons still stands behind Thorpe Station. The ARP Control was at first under the War Memorial, later moving to Heigham Grove, and then to purpose-built premises in Ipswich Road. The new drill hall in Wellesley Street, Kings Lynn, opened in 1936, was designed for dual-use as a gas and shrapnel-proof ARP station. We have seen how the ROC spotted for the air defence system, but other spotters also operated, albeit for different purposes. Many felt that production time was lost unnecessarily when air-raid warnings were sounded and workers immediately downed tools and made for the shelters. Often these were premature, or even false, alarms, so a number of firms sought a solution. Sometime in 1940, Boulton & Paul, LNER, Reckitt & Colman, Laurence, Scott & Electro-motors Ltd, and RJ Read Ltd, organised an air-raid-spotting rota from a tower erected in the grounds of 15 Bracondale and elsewhere, thus enabling work to continue after the sirens had sounded, and until there was a genuine need to take shelter.

Air defence in the Cold War

In the aftermath of World War II the prevailing feeling in Britain was one of insecurity. The polarisation of the Iron Curtain, the foundation of NATO, the blockade of Berlin and the Soviet acquisition of nuclear weapons all contributed, by 1950, to a heightened sense of vulnerability as confrontation between the two sides seemed inevitable. Impoverished as she was by World War II, Britain thus still felt it necessary to maintain and develop the luxury of the air defence system known as ROTOR, which included radar, AA guns, and the ROC.

Radar in Norfolk in the Cold War

The retention of the original CH stations at Stoke Holy Cross and West Beckham, and the GCI site at Neatishead, amongst others, ensured some continuity in the system. What was additional to the scheme was the construction of underground reinforced concrete bunkers to house new types of radar at the existing Trimingham *[122]*, Hopton and Neatishead sites, and a wholly new Sector Operations Centre [SOC] at

122. TRIMINGHAM: a plinth on which was mounted a Type 14 radar.

123. BAWBURGH: the Guard-house of the 1950s Sector Operations Centre which processed information from the radar sites; after ROTOR it became a sub-Regional emergency Seat of Government.

Bawburgh *[123]*. Trimingham was rebuilt as a centrimetric Early Warning radar station with an R1 bunker, opening in 1953. Two years later it housed the first operational Green Garlic Type 80 radar, whose prototype had been first erected at Bard Hill. Hopton, a CH Extra Low radar station was housed in an R2 bunker, whilst Neatishead, a GCI radar station, was given firstly an R12 surface bunker *[124]*, and subsequently a two-level, underground R3 bunker. The Bawburgh SOC was in an R4 three-level bunker. This was where all the information from the radars and the ROC posts was assembled, interpreted and synthesised in order that the appropriate action might be taken. Its central feature was a full-height operations-room, overlooked by cabins for the various controllers, and surrounded by telecommunications equipment, generators and offices. All these installations had the characteristic guard-room of the period, made to look like a domestic bungalow, usually housing the access tunnels and stairs to the underground bunkers. The radars were mounted on cubical concrete plinths or on steel gantries depending on the size and type being used. By the 1970s, new equipment meant that fewer sites were needed and only Neatishead has continued to receive each new radar equipment *[125]* as it was developed right up until the end of

124. NEATISHEAD: the R12 surface bunker at this radar station.

125. NEATISHEAD: the Type 84 Radar Scanner, the only such Cold War radar still to be mounted.

the Cold War. Along with Trimingham it is currently operational, handling AEW data, but also housing the Radar Museum. Trimingham holds mobile radar equipment under a radome *[126 &127]*. It was intended that Bawburgh would receive the RAF master control centre, but this was switched to West Drayton because of its close proximity to Heathrow, being combined with the [civilian] southern air-traffic control system. Bawburgh's characteristic bungalow guardhouse and semi-sunken three-level R4 bunker may still be seen next to the woodland burial site just off the A47, and its W/T station is less than a mile away on the other side of the Norwich by-pass *[128]*. A serious fire in the R3 underground bunker at Neatishead in 1966, necessitated the continued use of the World War II Happidrome, [R30] which, despite the tragic circumstances in which several local fire-fighters lost their lives, has had the happy result of preserving it as the basis of the museum, frozen in 1993, when

126. TRIMINGHAM: the radome, constructed out of irregular polygons of Kevlon, provides a permanent home for a Type 91 radar, replacing the previously mobile arrangement.

127. TRIMINGHAM: the characteristic Guard-house, minus its verandah but with additional dormer windows.

it was stood down. The principles of ground control interception were founded on the ability to vector fighter aircraft onto possible intruders, and this necessitated having a means whereby the fighter might accurately locate itself in order to respond to directional instructions. A network of VHF Fixers was established on the ground, and those in Norfolk were at Cockthorpe [TF973416] and Hemsby [TG491196]. The installation was normally no more than a hut on a concrete base, operated by WRAF personnel.

128. BAWBURGH: the Sector Operations Centre's detached Wireless Telegraphy station, now separated from the main site by the A47.

AA defences in the Cold War

Norwich remained a GDA into the 1950s but it would appear that no new gun-sites were built. However Weybourne AA Camp remained as a training facility, and the emplacements for its 5.25 inch dual-purpose AA/Coast Defence guns are still to be seen overlooking the sea behind the Muckleburgh military museum *[129]*. Until 1955, when AA Command was disbanded, emergency plans were based on the defence of potential targets such as airfields and radar stations by LAA units. In 1947 the former 78 HAA Regiment RA [TA] was re-constituted as the 284th Regiment with HQ in Great Yarmouth. After several

129. WEYBOURNE: one of the AA School's dual-purpose 5.25 inch HAA and coastal artillery gun-pits; the gun sat in the circular pit in a turret, whilst the flat-roofed building with the ventilator housed the engine-room.

130. STOKE HOLY CROSS: the Microwave Tower.

amalgamations, it became, in 1955, the 284th [The Kings Own Royal Regiment, Norfolk Yeomanry] LAA Regiment RA [TA] with HQ back in Norwich. One of its constituent units had been the 389th LAA Regiment RA [Norfolk Yeomanry] [TA] which had been re-constituted in 1947 in Swaffham, and 418th [M] HAA Regiment RA [Norfolk][TA]. This last unit was the successor to the coast artillery regiment which had manned East Anglian coast batteries. The planned integration of radar and AA defences is illustrated by the formation, in1952, of the 860th [M] AA Control & Reporting Battery RA [TA] at Neatishead, which later moved to Bawburgh, but had been disbanded by 1961. Airfield AA defences were also manned by the RAF Regiment. A mobile Type 87 AA Radar can be seen at the Muckleburgh museum.

By the 1960s, missiles, namely the Rapier and the Bloodhound, were replacing the guns as AA weapons. The first deployment of Bloodhound Mark1 surface-to-air missiles [SAM] was in eleven sites on the east coast, with two, Marham and Watton in Norfolk. These acted on information coming through Bawburgh SOC from the radar sites at Neatishead and Trimingham, using the new microwave towers, local examples being Stoke Holy Cross *[130]*, Tacolneston and Swaffham, into the Bloodhound Tactical Control Centre at Watton. The sites, each with pads for sixteen missiles, were built to a standard plan, with a large shed for arming and maintenance, Type 82 Orange Yeoman radar, Type 83 Yellow River radar, and the usual support buildings. This system operated from 1959 until 1963, sited to protect the V-bomber force, and the THOR IRBMs. The new, improved Bloodhound Mark II came into service in 1964, with West Raynham providing a new location. This also now became the location for the servicing and maintenance depot for the whole programme. The missile site itself had few permanent features as the system was meant to be mobile. Apart from skeleton towers for the Type 86 radar, and the concrete pads, little is visible. West Raynham's site is about to be [2008]

131. DOCKING: ORLIT B aircraft spotting post of the 1960s [TF671371].

destroyed and the site returned to agriculture. Bloodhound Mark II was deployed in eastern England until 1970 when it was removed to Germany as part of NATO's defences, and then back in England from 1975 until 1987, latterly dependent once more on Neatishead's Types 84 and 85 radars and the associated infrastructure. From the late-1960s the AA close-defence function was fulfilled by Rapier, a mobile system manned by the RAF Regiment, one squadron being based at West Raynham. Although the missile was launched from open sites, or ones at most protected by fieldworks, of which nothing remains, the surviving dome trainer or, more properly, the Air Defence Tactical Training Theatre [ADT3] is a structure of some distinction. The remarkable acoustic properties inside make 'theatre' a most appropriate descriptor.

The Royal Observer Corps in the Cold War

The ROC was reformed in early-1947 to provide an aircraft-spotting service as ever, but more closely integrated into the RAF's fighter control system. The wartime 16 Group, centred on Norwich was part of the RAF's Eastern Sector, and its HQ moved to RAF Old Catton, now on the Norwich ring-road. In 1953 it became 6 Group, with 17 clusters of posts under command, now 53 in all, with RAF Horsham St Faith becoming HQ of a new Eastern Area stretching from Ipswich north to Mablethorpe [Lincolnshire]. Reporting was to the Filter Plot at Watnall, with the RAF's local SOC at Bawburgh. As well as changes in the overall co-ordination of the service there were changes on the ground. In 1951, Messrs. Orlit, manufacturers of small concrete buildings had produced a ROC post which would become standard. It was a concrete box with a roofed section, and one open to the sky for mounting the new graduated post chart on its removable pillar. The post could either stand on the ground [Orlit A] or on concrete legs, 6 foot [1.9m] above the ground [Orlit B]. A very few posts were mounted on other buildings, built to different designs, or remained makeshift. An Orlit A post may be seen alongside the A148 road near Letheringsett, and Orlit B posts may be found at Old Buckenham and Docking *[131]*. Despite the presence of ROC posts such as that on top of Hunstanton lighthouse from 1953 to 1960, by the early-1950s, it was becoming apparent that the human eye, even aided by primitive sighting instruments was unequal to the task of identifying and tracking high-speed jet aircraft, and the future of the ROC was not bright. However, the need for a network of

132. NORWICH: the Royal Observer Corps semi-sunken control bunker on the ring-road at Old Catton, demolished as this book goes to press.

warning-posts to report on nuclear strikes and to track the movement of radiation or nuclear fall-out had been identified, and the ROC, combined with the old ARP service under the snappy title of United Kingdom Warning and Monitoring Organisation [UKWMO], was given the task. To enable them to carry out this new role, an underground post was designed, and between 1957 and 1964 some 1500 of these were constructed, if possible on existing sites. The post consisted of a concrete box, 19 feet by 8 foot 6 inches by 7 foot 6 inches [5.8 x 2.6 x 2.3m], with access through a hatch and down a ladder. Inside were a desk, a double-bunk and a chemical toilet. On the surface were the turret with hatch and Ground Zero Indicator, a ventilator, and the Fixed Survey Metre Probe. Each post had a crew of four, was in a cluster of three or four, and in telephone contact with ROC Group HQ. Many of the existing sites were re-sited in the1953 re-organisation, some because they would be unsuitable for sunken structures. In all, 29 were re-sited, that at Hunstanton descending to the cliff-top, with nine being re-named. At least four posts, Kings Lynn, Mundesley, Thetford and West Raynham were re-sited twice. The Gorleston post [16/T2] was moved about two miles [3km] south to the grounds of the Home Office Sector Operations Room in 1960, becoming Hopton [6/E3]. If the posts were to be protected, then so should the group HQs. Norwich was given a new semi-sunken HQ building of the standard design in 1961, on the RAF Old Catton site *[132]*, later

133. DERSINGHAM: ORLIT A aircraft post, and adjacent underground post, beautifully-restored and kept for occasional public viewing.

re-named Chartwell Road. It has a superstructure with ventilators on the surface, and a buried, double height operations room with a central well overlooked by balconies. The plotting table was up-dated by information coming in from the scattered posts and recorded on perspex panels by volunteers who became expert at mirror-writing. The Eastern Area HQ moved here in 1961 until 1966. Several ROC annual camps were located in Norfolk, in 1962 at Horsham St Faith, at West Raynham in 1963, twice at Watton in 1969 and 1970, and back at West Raynham in 1971. Many of the posts were culled in 1968, but the remainder, 32 including at least six from out of county, continued in service, along with the 6 Group HQ until stand-down came in 1991. Many of the underground posts survive in the county. That at West Raynham is unusual being built into the old airfield Battle HQ. Dersingham *[133]*, occasionally open to the public, has been preserved in pristine condition by Steve Marsh, a local enthusiast who has managed to re-equip it with all the instruments and other appropriate artefacts.

Maintaining the Infrastructure in the Cold War

Somewhat surprisingly, given the importance of the several radar stations, airfields, and other air defence installations in Norfolk, only four main roads were given strategic priority, the A11, the A47, the A140, and the A146, as Essential Services Routes. This meant that in the event of a nuclear strike, these routes would have been kept clear of refugees and non-essential traffic. The Military Road Route System of the 1970s and 1980s by-passed most of East Anglia, and Norfolk itself, altogether.

A network of Microwave Towers was erected by British Telecom from the 1950s, ostensibly to facilitate the transmission of colour television to the waiting nation but, in truth, wholly for the peacetime dissemination of signals intelligence, and general military communications in war. The network, often referred to as Backbone, sought to by-pass cities, where bombing might damage the underground cabling. A spur from the main north/south line, went through Peterborough via Swaffham to

134. FELTWELL: USAF radomes containing listening equipment.

Tacolneston and Stoke Holy Cross, with further links to Neatishead, Bawburgh, and Trimingham. Another element of the emergency communications network comprised the Hilltop radio stations, provided for the use of the armed forces, the police, and the emergency services. In Norfolk, there are examples at Tacolneston and at Bodham Hill. The prize for continuity, however, must go to Feltwell, a site first used in World War 1, was rebuilt in the 1930s, and which still continues in use as a USAF listening post *[134]*.

Despite the widespread death and destruction expected as the result of a nuclear exchange, efforts were made to protect society's infrastructure by constructing bunkers for both national and local government. In the event of a nuclear strike on the plethora of widespread targets, either legitimate or innocent, the nation would be ruled by regional commissioners located in Regional Seats of Government [RSG]. Norfolk came under Region 4 administered from RSG4 in Cambridge, but after ROTOR's demise, the Bawburgh SOC became available as a sub-RSG for Norfolk and Suffolk, sub-Region 4i. The 1961 Norfolk County Council Main emergency centre lies under the nine storeys of County Hall/Police HQ in Martineau Road, and has been regularly up-graded, but the County Stand-by, under a Social Services day centre in Grimston Road, Kings Lynn, had been abandoned by the 1980s. Broadlands District Council maintains a purpose-built bunker close to its Norwich offices, and Brecklands District Council retains its 1980s bunker in East Dereham in case it ever needs an Emergency Planning centre.

THE PROVISION OF LOGISTICAL SUPPORT 5

A nation's armed forces can only function effectively and efficiently if they have sufficient back-up in terms of supplies of food, fuel and materiel, if they have shelter against the elements, if they receive proper training, and if the leadership is well-organised and confident. Secondary requirements may include entertainment and social welfare. It has been argued that troops are more confident going into battle if they know that their own medical services will take care of them if they are injured, and that the enemy will treat them humanely if they are captured. This chapter examines all these topics which provide the framework within which feats of arms may be achieved. It looks at barracks, camps, depots and drill halls; at the use of requisitioned private premises for formation HQs; at training establishments; at munitions production; at medical facilities and hospitality; at organisational infrastructure including housing; and lastly at prisoner-of-war [PoW] camps.

Barracks, camps, and drill halls

At the beginning of the twentieth century Norwich was a military town. Nelson Cavalry Barracks was the permanent home of 12th Lancers, whilst Britannia Barracks, built as a result of the Cardwell reforms, was the local depot of the Norfolk Regiment, which in 1914 had one battalion in India, another in Ireland, and its 3rd [Reserve] Bn. at the depot. The Norfolk Yeomanry Cavalry, with an office in Erpingham House, was based in the drill hall in Cattlemarket Street, along with the TF engineers and Army Service Corps. The Norfolk Regiment's 4th Territorial Force [TF] Bn.had its HQ in the Chapelfields drill hall, the TF gunners were in Surrey Street Artillery Barracks [Ivory House], and the TF medics at Bethel Street. The Yeomanry and all the TF units had squadrons, companies and batteries spread across the county, meeting in a variety of venues to train, with the Norfolks' 5th TF Bn. centred on East Dereham. The enormous expansion of the army throughout World War I necessitated the construction of purpose-built hutted camps on a large scale, as well as examples of the adaptation of existing premises. The 6th [Cyclists] Bn. Norfolk Regiment had a company based in Thetford in 1914, and it may have been they who were billeted in Thetford Priory's Abbey Farm Barns, around four hundred years old, but serving as an army camp. Other, newer battalions of the Norfolks were raised in Norwich but quickly moved on to either established camps as was the 7th Bn, sent to Shorncliffe [Kent] in 1914, or to suitable wide open spaces under canvas, like the 3/4th and 3/5th Bns. sent to Windsor Great Park early in 1915, and then on to Halton Park, Tring [Hertfordshire], for their pre-embarkation training.

135. KINGS LYNN, Providence Street: the drill hall built in the late 1930s for the Anti-Tank regiment newly-formed from the Norfolk Yeomanry.

Between the wars, evidence of the great Expansion Period programme of building for the armed forces in the mid-1930s, is confined in Norfolk, mainly to the new airfields. However, the conversion of the Yeomanry to field artillery in 1920, and then, in 1938, into a specialist anti-tank regiment, made it necessary to acquire new premises for their HQ at Swaffham, and at Providence Street, Kings Lynn *[135]*. These provided vital new facilities both for training on the guns themselves, and for the storage of vehicles and equipment. A similar situation obtained in Norwich, where the field artillery's conversion to an AA regiment demanded a new drill hall on Aylsham Road, with a further new drill hall on Southtown Road, Great Yarmouth. The infantry were not left out with new drill halls in Aylsham *[136]*, Wymondham, Dersingham and Wellesley Street, Kings Lynn. Contemporary with these drill halls are the Mobilisation Stores, in which was stored brand new equipment, ready for issue to TA units if it proved necessary for them to be mobilised. Examples survive at Setchey [West Winch], Arminghall and at Fakenham. Many of these were specifically for the storage of AA guns, instruments and searchlights, and that at Arminghall was referred to as an AA Ordnance Depot, supplying ammunition to HAA and LAA sites around Norwich, whilst more general supplies were handled by the depot at Attleborough. Britannia Barracks continued in use as the Infantry Training Centre [ITC] for the numerous battalions of the Norfolk Regiment which would be formed during the course of World War II. Accommodation was also needed for troops on coast defence duties. The 2nd Bn. Cambridgeshire Regiment, for instance, was provided with a hutted camp on Stiffkey Marshes, later used as an AA practice camp, and now a holiday camping-site *[137]*.

136. AYLSHAM: the 1930s drill hall built for a company of territorials belonging to the Norfolk Regiment.

137. STIFFKEY: the Guard-house of the camp which housed the 2nd Bn. Cambridgeshire Regiment in the early part of WWII, and which then became an AA practice camp; it is now a holiday camp-site.

The great recruitment and mobilisation programme of World War I, was designed to produce an inexhaustible stream of reinforcements for [mainly] the Western Front. In World War II, there was a different scenario. Initially an army had to be gathered together as a defence against invasion. Then a large part of the RAF and the 8th USAAF had to be accommodated while they used East Anglia as their base for operations against occupied Europe, and then another army, much of it in transit from the USA, had to be formed and trained prior to the Allied invasion of France. The demand on land and buildings was enormous. Any large house with its parkland was greedily consumed by the armed services. A good example is the Walpole Estate at Mannington Hall and Wolterton Park. A RE Field Coy and a RA Field Bty were in residence in 1941; the next year the Household Cavalry had arrived; followed by the 49th Reconnaissance Regiment; whilst there was a searchlight battery in long-term occupation. The piggeries, we are told, were used by "war dogs", presumably in training for messenger or casualty recovery duties. In Hunstanton, the Sandringham Hotel, built in 1899 [now demolished], was requisitioned for a while as HQ for the Brigade of Guards. Next, Canadian troops were billeted there, and later on, it became home for the accounts department of the LNER, evacuated from London's bombs. The demand for unit and formation HQs was almost insatiable. Bayfield Hall near Holt was HQ for a succession of infantry

138. KETTERINGHAM HALL: this stately mansion built 1840-50, was Station 147- HQ 2nd Air Division 8th USAAF; it was surrounded by huts, and there was an open-air swimming-pool in front of the hall.

brigades: 53 Bde. in 1939, 222 Bde. from 1940 until June 1942, then 220 Bde, until 1943, with its HQ in the Ball-room. Similar functions were performed by Docking Hall, Cockley Cley Hall, Ingham Old Hall, Watlington Hall and many others. Rackheath Hall, Haveringland Hall

[Swannington] and Blickling Hall [Oulton Street] all served as officers' messes for nearby airfields; Ketteringham Hall [Station147] *[138]*, a house of 1840-50 with extra hutted accommodation in the grounds, was HQ 2nd Air Division 8th USAAF. Most traces of these temporary occupations have now all but disappeared, a blink of the eye in the long history of these ancient houses. Bylaugh Hall *[139]*, a grand house of c1850, and HQ of the RAF's 100 Group with cellars used as operations rooms, was

139. BYLAUGH HALL: this mid-Victorian house, recently restored from a state of ruin, was HQ RAF 100 Group, with operations rooms in the cellars.

described as a ruin in Pevsner's 1962 Norfolk volume of his Buildings of England series, and its 1990s up-date. Not only has the house been restored, but there are visible reminders of its wartime life in the Braithwaite tank on its skeleton tower, pump-house *[140]*, and various temporary-brick, Nissen and timber huts in the grounds. Hedenham Hall, north of Bungay, now converted into apartments, was a rest

140. BYLAUGH HALL: the Braithwaite tank on its tower and pump-house.

centre for aircrew. Between 1942 and 1943, RAF Old Catton became Camp Thomas [Station 108], HQ of the USAAF 2nd Bombardment Wing, having served in the Battle of Britain as a detached Operations Block for RAF Coltishall. The remaining building is now HQ of the Norfolk & Suffolk Air Training Corps. Stratton Strawless Hall also served as Coltishall's other reserve Operations Block.

Depots

The operations of the 8th USAAF required extensive supply and storage support. At Earsham [Station 545] there was the main bomb dump, but the principal stores complex was at Eccles [Station 548] on the north-west perimeter of Snetterton Heath airfield. Here were three T2 hangars *[141]* plus other storage buildings, and 14 hard-standings for aircraft, although 26 were projected. Neaton [Station 505], at Griston on the south-east side of Watton airfield was the main air depot. Again, a group of three T2 hangars was supplemented by other

141. SNETTERTON: one of the T2 hangars of the Eccles Road depot.

large storage buildings and a MT park. The airfield had two extra B1 and two Blister hangars for carrying out repairs to aircraft. The supply of fuel was always a problem but the pipeline from Stanlow on the Mersey, across to Misterton near Scunthorpe and on down to Sandy in Bedfordshire kept the aircraft aloft. Local cell depots held supplies from which to top up the tanks on the airfields themselves. The Air Ministry had a fuel depot on Mundford Road, Thetford, and there was a Petrol Depot at Ellingham

142. ELLINGHAM: the guard-house of the petrol depot, now grain silos.

[142]. The Thetford depot is still operational, reputedly supplying Lakenheath. The line of the pipeline is marked by white-painted stile-like structures at regular intervals along the roadside verge, at right-angles to the carriage-way. All sorts of other stores were held in either general or specialist storage facilities. There was a general equipment depot at Norwich, and Happisburgh and Hopton were the RAF's experimental radar depots, for instance. The former Harling Road airfield became a store for the army, and then a tank-repair facility for the US army. Bomb and ammunition supply and storage posed as big a problem as did fuel. Pulham's redundant great airship hangar was seen as an obvious place to store munitions- too obvious, as it was attacked twice in one week in June 1940, so munitions were stored in thirty-six sheds served by standard-gauge railway. The hangar was restricted to holding salvaged aircraft parts for re-use, although remaining a Reserve Ammunition Depot handling SAA and Pyrotechnics. The main munitions storage facility for East Anglia was Barnham, just over the Suffolk border from Thetford, but there was a Forward Ammunition Depot [FAD], run by 231 MU, at Hockering, opened in January 1943, five months behind schedule, holding the standard capacity of 8.4 kilotons of HE bombs, 840 tons of incendiaries in huts, and a total of 40,000 square feet [4,800 sq.m] for stacking SAA. At a remote and safer distance from all this, three huts were used for storing the shells for the Home Guard's Smith gun. The Guardroom, Fire

143. HOCKERING: the Technical Site of the RAF ammunition depot.

Station and MT Section *[143]* all remain, along with other buildings of the Technical Site, on Stone Lane, whilst in the adjacent woods, now protected as a SSSI, can be traced the concrete roads which linked the underground storage-bunkers, and a Nissen guard-room at the entrance *[144]*.

144. HOCKERING: the Nissen guard-house of the woodland ammunition depot.

After 1945, Hockering continued in service with satellite dumps on the airfields at Old Buckenham, Shipdham, Rackheath and Attlebridge. In 1958, Pulham, as 53 MU, took responsibility for the bomb storage on Seething and Bungay airfields. Barnham stayed in service, and in 1950 held stocks of the nuclear weapons which would be issued to East Anglian bases, including Marham and Watton, in the event of the possibility of war breaking out. Once the bulky Blue Danube had been superseded by more compact weapons, Marham was provided with its own atomic bomb-store on-site. The USAF retained Earsham as its FAD, with North Pickenham, Tuddenham and Little Snoring as satellites. Two of these were to become THOR bases. Possibly taking advantage of the generous hangar accommodation at Foulsham, 99 MU, operated a Mechanical Transport Reception facility there. At a day-to-day level, during World War II, a network of petrol supplies was identified for use in emergency situations, particularly in case of invasion. Selected petrol pumps around the county were designated for use, with keys being held by local RASC units. An example is the Fox Brothers' Central Cycle Stores in New Buckenham, with its manual petrol pump. The Admiralty also maintained a network of armament and supply depots. Scant remains of one such remain in Waveney Forest near the Round-house, where the Beccles to Norwich railway line was used to transport ammunition and explosives, which would be unloaded for dispersed storage on hard-standings. The remains of a camp, a large Emergency Water Supply tank with its controlling valves, and other depot infrastructure including weapons pits may be found in the bracken.

During the Cold War, food and fuel were stockpiled for distribution in an emergency, as were vehicles for emergency use. There were, for example, MAFF Buffer Depots in Station Road, Thetford and in Kings Lynn, and RAF Watton housed a Home Office Supply & Transport depot, holding trucks for the emergency distribution of food, and vehicles such as Green Goddess fire-engines for Civil Defence use.

Training

Mousehold Heath outside Norwich was the traditional cavalry training area throughout the nineteenth century, and it probably continued in such use in at least the early days of World War I, as recruits flocked to the colours. We have already seen how several Norfolk airfields carried out training functions: The School of Air-fighting at Sedgeford, then at Bircham Newton, and the School of Navigation and Bomb-dropping at Snarehill [Thetford]. Maybe this last designation is a clue to the sophistication of the activity, not yet an exact science. Sedgeford pilots used the bombing range at Thornham Marsh. Towards the end of World War I, Feltwell and Harling Road were both established as Training Depot Stations. There are many rifle-ranges, which were used by the VTC, or by new recruits to the army. Some are still in use, and some can be traced back to the Rifle Volunteers of Victorian times.

Norfolk really came into its own as a training area with World War II. The Stanford Battle Training Area [STANTA], also

145. THETFORD FOREST: a set of buffers, a stone's-throw from the A134 marking the rail-head which served the tank-training area [TL854868].

known as the Breckland Area, was set up in 1942, to provide a large area of training land for the forces preparing for the Second Front. On 13th June 1942, residents of the villages of West Tofts, Tottington and Stanford, many of them tenants of Lord Walsingham's Merton Estate, were given one week to leave their homes with what they could carry, and without compensation. Also included in the training area were the de-populated settlements of Langford, Sturston, and Buckenham Tofts. North of Thetford was a tank-training area. Close to where the new power-station now stands on the Mundford road, there were railway sidings where tanks could be loaded and unloaded. A number of concrete ramps and buffers *[145]* survive near the level-crossing. The battle area is still in use, served by Bodney Camp, and now takes in the disused airfields of Watton, East Wretham and Bodney. A few years ago, former residents were allowed in for a day to see what

146. THETFORD, Snarehill: the quadrant tower on the World War II bombing range [TL901814].

147. SNETTISHAM: a row of AT blocks, presumably part of the 1940 anti-invasion defences, subsequently adapted by US troops for mounting machine-guns [hence the numbers painted on them]; the area had become an AA training camp and firing range.

remained of their childhood homes. The old Snarehill airfield became a bombing decoy, and then a bombing range. Alongside the decoy blockhouse stands a two-storey quadrant tower *[146]*, from which observers would inform pilots of the accuracy of their bombing. Another bombing range at North Wootton, north of Kings Lynn, was used by 17OTU based at Steeple Morden and Upwood [Cambridgeshire]. The north Norfolk coast was busy with anti-aircraft training. In summer 1936, the School of AA Gunnery was established at Weybourne, using targets towed by aircraft from Bircham Newton, and also radio-controlled Queen Bees. A whole range of AA weapons was fired from here including 3.7 inch HAA, Bofors LAA guns and Z battery 3 inch un-rotated rocket projectiles. The emplacements for 5.25 inch dual-purpose CD and AA guns may still be seen. AA training continued from here and from Stiffkey Marshes until 1958 under the auspices of No.1 Anti-Aircraft Practice Camp. The camp is now home to the Muckleburgh Collection and some of the original huts remain, as do some at Stiffkey. There was also a Z-battery range for the

Home Guard at Heacham, and the USAAF had an AA gunnery school at Snettisham *[147]*. Here they used existing AT Blocks as weapons mounts, but the narrow-gauge railway on site was put in later for gravel-extraction rather than target-towing. Dotted across the county are rifle-ranges used by the Home Guard, including Fritton, Horsford, Matlaske, Kimberley, Hingham, Thetford [Olleys Farm], and near Diss, Wortham Ling [Suffolk]. The Thetford Home Guard used Bridge House, with its extensive outbuildings, for its training. The 2i/c, whose home it was, wisely confined training with sticky bombs to the gardens, and drill to the Maltings Yard opposite. As priorities changed once the threat of invasion had receded, so facilities were put to new use. When 125 AT Regiment quit Catton Hall *[148]* for its ill-fated deployment to Singapore, the park became a tented training camp for 76 Division personnel, with officers' accommodation in the White House, and NAAFI provision in the Village Hall.

148. OLD CATTON HALL, Norwich: used as a hospital in World War I; early in World War II it first provided a base for a territorial AT unit from Sunderland, and then it became an army training camp.

149. HOLME-next-the-SEA: one of several blockhouses which housed the gear for winching targets along rails on this tank-gunnery range [TF711449].

The north Norfolk coast was also used for training in armoured vehicles. On Titchwell Marshes there are range block-houses which housed the machinery for running targets along rails for the tanks to fire at *[149]*. These were used by a number of armoured units including the 4/7th Dragoon Guards, 13/18th Hussars, 27th Lancers, and the Westminster Dragoons, [2nd County of London Yeomanry]. They used Firefly tanks, mounting the new 17 pounder AT gun. Brancaster Beach made a unique contribution to the preparations for D-Day. In 1943, the planning for the Normandy landings, was being undertaken in the knowledge that the invading troops, British, American and Canadian in the main, would come up against the most heavily-defended coastline in the history of warfare. In order to be able to deal with the beach obstacles and fixed defences, Major-General Hobart, one of the pioneers of armoured warfare, was given the job of both developing specialised armoured vehicles, and of training their crews to clear the beaches. He set up 79th Armoured Division to carry out this task with, what were known as his "funnies", adaptations of tanks which could clear minefields, bridge dykes or remove obstructions. Much of their training was carried out in Suffolk. Strangely enough, it was not the German fortifications of the Atlantic Wall which presented the particular problem which only a Norfolk beach could solve, but a natural phenomenon. So thorough were the planners in their attention to detail and in their determination that unnecessary casualties might not be suffered, that geologists were consulted over the likely consistency of the landing beaches. The answer came back that there was a strong possibility that some of the British target beaches between Ouistreham and Arromanches might contain strips of soft blue clay, which could present problems to armoured vehicles attempting to cross them. Commandos landed surreptitiously on some of these beaches, bringing back samples for analysis, and the geologists duly found their suspicions confirmed. The only beach in Britain with a similar geological make-up was at Brancaster, and here, Hobart's assault engineers, by trial and error, developed and tested the vehicle which would overcome this hazard. One of the established "funnies" was the Armoured Vehicle Royal Engineers [AVRE], one version of which was a tank body with two large prongs on the front, normally used for dropping large fascines into ditches. For this particular task, mounted between the prongs was a drum carrying a carpet of coir and scaffolding poles. This could be rolled out in a long strip, allowing a convoy of vehicles to follow along behind without sinking into the blue clay, and on the day it worked a treat. The mine-detonating device 'Roly-Poly', consisting of massive iron rollers pushed ahead of a Churchill AVRE, was also tested at Brancaster. Withdrawn from Italy in December 1943, the 7th Armoured Division was stationed in Norfolk in order to prepare for the Normandy landings. Divisional HQ with junior and senior messes was in Didlington Hall. The Queen's Brigade was billeted around the Kings Lynn area, whilst 22nd Armoured Brigade occupied hutted camps between Ickburgh and Hilborough in Thetford Forest: 1RTR at Sugar Hill, 5RTR in Shakers Wood, and 4th County of London Yeomanry [Sharpshooters], in High Ash Camp. Their HQ was a few miles to the north, in Cockley Cley Hall, with the officers occupying the big house, whilst other ranks were billeted at North Lodge, 400 yards north-east of the Hall. The lay-out of the camps can still be seen in Thetford Forest where a Cromwell IV tank stands as a memorial beside the A1065, and a trail has been laid out passing the hut-bases of the living-quarters and the REME workshops. A Nissen hut has been restored to give a flavour of the camp *[150]*.

150. THETFORD FOREST: a reconstructed Nissen hut billet on the site of one of 7th Armoured Division's camps during the months leading up to D-Day.

Munitions production in World War 1

Aircraft were manufactured in a number of places in Norfolk during World War I. The largest manufacturer was Boulton & Paul of Norwich who, from 1915, operated their large factory with adjacent flying field for test-flying aircraft, at Mousehold on Salhouse Road. The factory had seven triple aircraft sheds with bowstring roofs, plus double and single GS hangars, two of which survive, along with some gabled sheds from this date. Also in Norwich, were Mann Egerton's, who built aircraft from a large hangar on Cromer Road, which was only removed in 1984. In Kings Lynn, Savages better known as fairground builders, manufactured aircraft which were tested on a field to the north of the town, and the St Nicholas Ironworks assembled aircraft whose components had been made elsewhere. More important than aircraft, were the explosives needed to feed the guns on the Western Front. In the absence of conventional ingredients some improvisation was necessary, and HM Acetone Factory established in 1916 in Queen Alexandra Dock, was forced to fall back on horse chestnuts, gathered in thousands of tons by the local children, from woods including those on the Sandringham

Estate. Caley's St James Works in Norwich were used to making Christmas Crackers, but switched their production to explosives. Their female operatives, exposed to cordite, were known as the Norwich Canaries. Many manufacturers of agricultural commodities could change easily to the war economy. Barnard's Norfolk Ironworks had contracts from the War Office and the Admiralty for large quantities of barbed wire, and Cranes of Dereham made almost 25000 wheels for field-guns. The boot and shoe industry also had a big part to play. Haldinsteins, Edwards & Holmes, and Sextons between them produced half a million pairs of boots and shoes for the forces. Fulfilling more specialist work, Howlett & White made thigh-length sheepskin boots for the RFC/RAF, and also special boots for French and Russian troops including some for the Cossacks. Many clothing firms secured military contracts, Chamerlins of Botolph Street, for instance made uniforms for both the armed services and for Royal Ordnance Factory employees. They were the sole manufacturers of their Pegamoid water-proof clothing.

After the war, everything returned to normal. Boulton & Paul continued to build aircraft, and some of their Norwich-built Sidestrand bombers were based at Bircham Newton in 1929. The factory continued until 1936, when the aircraft-building part of the company's operation was moved to Pendeford, Wolverhampton, taking much of its work-force with it.

Munitions production World War II

Although no longer concentrating their aircraft-building in Norwich, Boulton & Paul took up in 1939, where they had left off in 1936. At their Riverside Works, and on Salhouse Road they produced a wide range for the war effort including wooden fuselages for Oxford bomber-trainers, body and nose sections for Horsa gliders, and a number of structures for use on airfields. These included hangars for aircraft factories and RAF Armament Training Schools. The VR1 & VR2 [4178/44] hangars were single-span sheds with gabled roofs, the double version having no dividing wall. Examples can still be seen at Stormy Down [Glamorgan], and Evanton [Ross & Cromarty]. A hangar built for Ipswich airport has been moved and re-erected at Flixton Air Museum [Suffolk]. It would also appear likely that they designed and manufactured steel-framed hutting, possibly including the corrugated-iron-clad gabled Jane hut. They also produced Somerfield track for grass airfields, air-raid shelters, and tank-transporters. Although the Riverside Works has been completely cleared away, their Mousehold site on Salhouse Road retains two bowstring-roofed hangars, and one smaller hangar like that removed from Narborough, dating from World War I, and extensive sheds on the sites and alignments of those producing aircraft in 1920s-1940s. Part of the site is now occupied by MSI Defence, and the rest is an industrial estate. As in World War I, local firms such as FW Harmers of St Andrews Street, Heigham,

Norwich producing uniforms, and Dereham's Hobbies factory were harnessed to the war effort. Barnards on Rackheath Road made aircraft parts and shells. Other companies continued peace-time production but working to Utility Goods designs using minimal materials. It must be remembered that counties such as Norfolk made their biggest contribution to the Nation's well-being through the maximisation of agricultural production. The Women's Land Army, 80 000-strong nationally by 1943, maintained a large contingent of 1600 in Norfolk.

Large numbers of trawlers were requisitioned by the Admiralty and converted as minesweepers and coastal convoy escorts, but the Ministry of Agriculture & Fisheries exerted pressure for at least some of these to be returned to fishing as food was in such short supply. One solution was for the local ship-building yards to produce specialist boats to carry out the duties hitherto performed by the impressed trawlers.

Pleasure-craft builders such as Herbert Woods of Potter Heigham, HJ Percival of Horning, and Graham Bunn of Wroxham built Motor Launches [MLs] and other small specialist craft for the Navy. At Great Yarmouth, motor-fishing vessels for RN use were built by Woods. Fellows & Co. assembled small landing-craft, and repairs to RN vessels were carried out by the intriguingly named Crabtree 1931.

151. NORWICH, 44 Bethel Street: the frontage of the drill hall, formerly a skating-rink, requisitioned by the TF in 1908 as a base for the 2nd East Anglian Divisional Field Ambulance RAMC; by 1931 their successor unit had moved to Ivory House.

Hospitals, medical facilities and welfare

In World War I, large numbers of wounded soldiers returning from action for treatment or convalescence, required more resources than either the existing private or voluntary systems could provide. The RAMC units of the TF, like those based at Bethel Street in Norwich *[151]*, were designed to travel with their parent divisions on active service. The TF also organised General Hospitals and Clearing Hospitals, with 500 beds in each, but the local ones were in Cambridge and Ipswich respectively, and many of their personnel would have been shipped out to the Front. The Norwich Regimental Depot at Britannia Barracks had been provided with one of the new pattern of hospital in 1886, but this was little more than a sick-bay. The War Office had drawn up plans for hutted hospitals to be erected in the grounds of existing hospitals and asylums, or of country

152. THORPE ST ANDREW, Norwich: the Asylum which became the Norwich War Hospital in 1915.

houses. The Cambridge hospital, built on college sports grounds was designed by Charles Skipper [might he have been part of the famous Norwich architectural practice?] Using their organisational ability and the extensive web of volunteers, many of them from the Voluntary Aid Detachments [VADs], the Red Cross helped to set up a network of hospitals throughout the county. The County Asylum at Thorpe St Andrew, built in 1811 with several additions in the1840s and now converted into apartments, became, in April 1915, the Norfolk War Hospital *[152]*, from whence were co-ordinated the activities of some fifty auxiliary hospitals across the county. Examples included the former Hackford and Whitwell parochial school at Reepham, now the junior school, Old Catton Hall, as well as the Bishop's Palace, Bracondale, and the Carrow Auxiliary hospitals. At Lakenham, the former Council School in Hospital Lane, now an infants' school, served as a military hospital.

On the outbreak of war in 1939 there had been no increase in the small number of beds in military hospitals, but a recognition that air-raids would produce large numbers of civilian casualties, led to the setting up of the war Emergency Medical Service [EMS] to provide hospitals to treat all casualties alike. Once again, hutted hospitals were constructed, like that at Wymondham *[153*

153. WYMONDHAM: a Nissen hut, the only one now remaining of the USAAF hospital, now Wymondham College.

&154], handed over by the EMS in 1943 as the 77th USAAF Hospital. Now absorbed into Wymondham College, only the water tower, one Nissen hut former ward, and an administrative block in temporary brick, survive. As in World War I, the Red Cross established a network of convalescent and auxiliary hospitals including Blofeld Hall, Felthorpe Hall and Hardingham Hall, in Norwich, Broome Place, Ditchingham Hall, Cranmer Hall, Fakenham, Denton House, Harleston, Hilborough Hall, Thetford, Stow Hall, Kings Lynn, Pickenham Hall, Swaffham, Salle Hall, Reepham, and Wroxham Hall. The old naval hospital in Great Yarmouth, in use as a naval asylum, was evacuated to Lancaster in 1939 for the duration, fortunately for its inmates who would have otherwise been amongst the considerable number of casualties when it was bombed. Earlham Hall, now part of UEA, also served as a hospital, and one hut remains, now a café *[155]*.

Hospitality

Wherever there were soldiers away from home, a number of charitable organisations would open canteens and clubs to offer alternatives to the more traditional pursuits of servicemen at a loose end. In November

154. WYMONDHAM: the Water Tower of the USAAF hospital.

155. NORWICH, Earlham Hall: a hut from the US military hospital, now in use as a café.

1915, the YMCA opened a hut in Park Road, Hunstanton. In World War II, the Linton White Institute in Salle, now the village hall, became a NAAFI canteen. In Norwich, as well as the Salvation Army in St Giles, there was a NAAFI Club built on a bomb-site in Rampant Horse Street. The commercial sector also did its bit. The Samson & Hercules ball-room in Tombland was given over to US servicemen three nights a week, whilst the Empire Cinema in Great Yarmouth put on special programmes for servicemen and women. The WVS provided canteens for the sailors in Great Yarmouth when they came ashore, and for those who were billeted in the town whilst training or crewing shore establishments.

The military infrastructure

We have already seen how many country-houses were taken over by the army for camps and headquarters, and by the air forces for headquarters and messes. On the coast, similar demands on space were being made by the Royal Navy. Great Yarmouth was home to several distinct naval establishments. The original shore base was HMS Watchful, fronted onto the River Yare,

156. WAVENEY FOREST: the interior of one of eight underground chambers, presumably for the storage of munitions and equipment, and possibly related to the activities of British Resistance Organisation personnel, known to have been centred nearby. The corrugated-iron shuttering of the roof can be seen along with iron stanchions and chicken-wire revetment of the earth walls. [photo: AGK]

at a point level with Southtown Station and Wellington Pier. Here its fifty or so trawlers and drifters berthed, and its HQ was in the Walrond Institute until that was bombed, when it moved to the naval hospital. The minesweeper base, HMS Miranda was a little way downstream, with its HQ in an old sailing-barge called the Mehalah, moored at the Fishwharf. The base for MLs and MTBs, three flotillas with around two dozen boats all told, HMS Midge was about a mile down-stream with officers' quarters in Shaddingfield Lodge at the naval hospital. The PWSS was on Gorleston Pier at the mouth of the Yare, with fuel tanks, a naval canteen, and a gunnery school, all in the South Denes. In the north of the town were billets for WRNS and for some of the overspill from Lowestoft's big training base, HMS Europa. Also in Great Yarmouth was 24 MCU of the RAF operating three high-speed launches for air-sea-rescue work. The boats were moored in the River Yare, whilst their crews were billeted in the Cliff Hotel. Also at Gorleston were the eight rescue launches of 60 RML [RN], and a RAF mine-laying detection unit which covered the coast between Harwich and Immingham. The PLA operated salvage tugs berthed on ABC Wharf in the River Yare, with HQ at the Nelson Garage. At Wells-next-the-Sea, on the north Norfolk coast was another RAF air-sea rescue unit, 23 MCU, with two seaplane-tenders and a pinnace. Their crews were billeted in an old cinema.

Military housing

There are good examples of RAF housing from the 1920s through to the post-World War II period at Bircham Newton, Coltishall, Watton and West Raynham, where houses have recently come onto the market. The military authorities have always acquired housing as necessary as in Hunstanton, for instance when the War Office requisitioned 80 houses for military personnel. By 1958, over 250 US families from the Sculthorpe base were accommodated in rented housing in the town, bringing much-needed income. Crew-quarters at Sculthorpe had been made of pre-fabricated hutting, but towards the end of the 1950s, the British Government provided conventional housing for US personnel, paid for by sales of surplus US tobacco, hence the houses were known as "tobacco houses".

Prisoner-of-War Camps

In both wars there were PoW camps in Norfolk. Many of them in World War I were work details based on industrial buildings or farms, and in no way looking anything like the popular image of a PoW camp with wire fences and guard-towers. In World War II, there were at least eleven in the county, numbered 52, 131 and 132, 173, 200, 231, 253, 255, 258, 271 and 272. Some of these camps fitted the popular image, but many others were more like refugee camps or transit camps for displaced persons, several at the end of the war being located on recently-vacated airfields where hutting was available. Camps 131 and 132 at Uplands, Diss, and Kimberley Park respectively, were agricultural work-camps for Italian PoWs. After VE Day, many under-used airfields served as PoW camps, Seething, for instance accommodating German prisoners awaiting repatriation. Some Nissen huts remaining at Cockley Cley Hall probably represent the former PoW Camp.

SITE GAZETTEER

NOTES

1 This is a list only of representative examples, surviving at time of compilation, not a complete inventory, unless specifically stated;

2 Where National Grid References are given, they are either 6-figure, and therefore only approximate, or else four figure references giving merely the km. square[s];

3 Drawing or Type Numbers used in several places show sequence/year of production: thus the Watch Office for All Commands was built to the 343rd design to emerge from the Air Ministry drawing office in 1943- hence 343/43.

4 Where building materials are given 'tb' is temporary brick ie: single brick's thickness plus buttresses; proprietary brands of hut eg Nissen or British Concrete Federation [BCF]

Chapter 1
Anti-invasion defence

The Coastal Crust

TF589241 Kings Lynn coast defence battery: BOP, magazine, gun-houses etc.

TF527253 Walkers Marsh: 3-bay pillbox with LAA mount

TF555234 Balaclava Farm: Home Guard store

TF674257 Castle Rising: rail-sockets & AT block on stream crossing

TF662368 Heacham south beach: four AT blocks and two AT gun-houses, one a Type 28 with spigot mortar thimble alongside, the other a modified Type 28a

TF699435 Holme: two pairs of spigot mortars and Home Guard store, with a Type 28 AT gun-house on approach road to beach

TF676420 Hunstanton: lighthouse & coastguard tower with naval pillbox, mark site of coast defence battery & Y Service listening post

TF651334 Snettisham: AT blocks and Home Guard store

TF770450 Brancaster: pillboxes, spigot mortar & remains of coast defence battery

TF873/8 440 Holkham: AT blocks and rails

TF878/9 441/2 Holkham: two double mg pillboxes, two more at TF891/2 443

TF894439 Holkham: Allan Williams turret

TF750446/8 Titchwell Marsh: two loop-holed structures enfilading beach

TF914441 Wells: two double mg pillboxes

TG183404 Aylmerton: WW1 circular pillbox

TG048444 Cley Eye: Allan Williams turret & pillbox on site of coast defence battery

TG209421 Cromer: L-shaped section post

TG09 43/4 Weybourne: group of mg posts and pillboxes

TG157431 Sheringham: AT blocks in Station car-park

TG098433 Weybourne: gun-house and OP

TG10.43 Muckleburgh: pillboxes WW1 & WW2 + spigot mortar etc.

TG132432 and TG127435/6 Weybourne: mg pillbox and two other pillboxes

TG295377 & 297380 Gimingham: 2 hexagonal pillboxes with LAA Hazzard mounts

TG34.34 Bacton: four pillboxes & L-shaped section post

TG35.33 Broomholm Priory: pillbox built into priory ruins + others around site

TG36/7 30/1 Happisburgh: coast defence battery & assorted pillboxes

TG40.28/9 Eccles & Hempstead: three pillboxes

TG422270 Sea Palling: circular WW1 pillbox

TG300372 Mundesley: coast defence battery

TG507174 Hemsby: double mg post and AT blocks on beach

TG49.19 Winterton: coast defence battery [BOP in lighthouse] and AT blocks

TG53.02 Gorleston: bungalows used by Links coast defence battery

Waveney Forest: underground storage chambers *[156]*

GHQ Line: River Great Ouse, Downham Market, and Pophams Eau

Brandon Creek: Type 28a AT gun-house and Type 22 pillbox at TL609919 & 614914

Hilgay: two Home Guard stores at TL618985 & 622987; pillbox at 630983, and spigot mortar at TL620988

TL60.97 Ten Mile Bank: Type 28a AT gun-house, 3 pillboxes and spigot mortar TF546009, 554009 & 507003 three Type 28a AT gun-houses; TF 554013 a Type 28 AT gun-house; TF586009, 575014, 583016, 574012, 556014, 559011, 537008, 552009, 519006, 528007 & 565011 all Type 24 shell-proof pillboxes; TF551007 & 557009 two Home Guard stores, along Pophams Eau between Downham Market & Three Holes.

TF599033 & 595030 Downham Market: two spigot mortars

TF602070 Stowbridge: AT pimples

Middle Level Drain

TF553069 Neeps Bridge: Home Guard store

TF540/2 048 Mortons Bridge: Home Guard store and spigot mortar

TF587139 Wiggenhall St Mary: spigot mortar near sluice

TF566118 Lordsbridge: pillbox at Rosary Farm, Mill Basin

Corps Line A Burnham Market to Beccles

TF90 37 Egmere: three type 24 pillboxes, two spigot mortars and a Home Guard store at cross-roads

TF899358 Barsham: pillbox in hedge-line

TF994259 Guist Hill: pillbox and
TF999137 Guist Green: spigot mortar

TG02 18 Mill Street, River Wensum: AT blocks and spigot mortars

TG072178 Pockthorpe, River Wensum: AT blocks

TG140137 Ringland, River Wensum: AT blocks and Home Guard store

TG245068 Old Bungay Road, Norwich: spigot mortar

TG319022 Hellington: type 22 pillbox

TM364978 & 360991 Loddon: pillboxes, and Home Guard stores behind drill hall

TM39.97 Raveningham: pillbox and several spigot mortars

TM44.96 Haddiscoe: three spigot mortars

Corps Line B Kings Lynn to Harleston

TF670135 High Bridge: two AT rail sockets & Home Guard store at TF671144

TF764144 Narford Hall: 36+ AT rails around bridge over R. Nar

TF748138 River Nar, two pillboxes

TF816095 Swaffham: pillbox by railway

TF832091 Swaffham: Pillbox by former railway-bridge

TF888070 North Pickenham: pillbox near railway-bridge

TF922011 Watton: pillbox near church

TG063955 Besthorpe: pillbox built onto end of house

TG142875 Tibbenham: pillbox south of airfield

TM197861 Pulham Market: loop-holed wall near church

TM245833 Harleston: pillbox in front garden of house plus spigot mortars
NB this Line continues on through Suffolk to the coast;

Line F1 River Ant

TG213357 Hanworth: half a circular WW1 pillbox

TG241/2 354 Gunton Station: two circular WW1 pillboxes

TG272334 & 296313 Bradfield & North Walsham: 2 circular WW1 pillboxes

TG325272 Honing: Type 24 pillbox; others at Dilham & Smallburgh

TG393261 Ingham: loop-holed wall

TG308295 & 307298 North Walsham: two circular WW1 pillboxes

TG310294 & 310298 North Walsham: mg post and Type 22 pillbox

TG300307 Spa Common: D-shaped WW1 pillbox

TG34 24 Wayford Bridge: circular WW1 pillbox , WW2 pillbox + spigot mortars

TG372172 Ludham Mill: loop-holed windmill and spigot mortar

Line FII Blakeney to Great Yarmouth

TG044426 Wiveton: pillbox at bridge over stream

TG060388 Letheringsett: spigot mortars and Home Guard store

TG091344 Edgefield: spigot mortar

TG191290 Ingworth WW1 circular pillbox

TG19.26 Aylsham: two large hexagonal pillboxes

TG199276 Aylsham: rectangular pillbox of concrete sacks onto end of water-mill

TG215254 Burgh-next-Aylsham: eight AT blocks at bridge

TG225240 Brampton: pillbox and six AT blocks

TG237228 Buxton: AT blocks

TG251216 Horstead: AT blocks

TG265199 Coltishall: pillbox on river-bank

TG403105 Acle: pillbox built onto end of Manor House

TG395116 & 398112 Fishley: two pillboxes

TG407105 & 409100 east of Acle: two pillboxes

TG506090 alongside A47 road: two WW1 hexagonal pillboxes

TG442090 Stracey Arms Windmill formerly loop-holed

TG418073 Halvergate: loop-holed barn on Tunstall road

Line FIII Norwich to Lowestoft

TG288070 Postwick: half-pillbox built onto barn on river-bank

TM45.98/99 St Olaves: WW1 pillbox, three WW2 pillboxes, rail-block, loop-holed wall, and three spigot mortars guarding two crossings

Auxiliary Unit areas of operation

Kings Lynn [centre, Dersingham, Brandon & Rougham], East Dereham, Brancaster, Walsingham, Kirkby Beedon, Norwich, Mautby and North Walsham

There are two OBs in Waveney Forest which were linked operationally with those on the neighbouring Somerleyton estate.

Chapter 2 The defence of vulnerable points

Airfield defences

Bircham Newton: hexagonal pillboxes at TF776340 & 784337

Bodney: pillboxes at TL830994, 840999, 844992 [+BHQ], 846994, & TF833001

Coltishall: four assorted pillboxes + defence posts around airfield

Docking: pillboxes at TF781392 & 786397

East Wretham: two double mg posts, two pillboxes, and SAA store at TG91.89

Feltwell: BHQ and square pillboxes at TL702904, 706896, 702887, and 702886

Foulsham: pillbox at TG036271

Hethel: strong-point with mg pits and SAA store at TG153017

Horsham St Faith: octagonal pillbox at TG228130

Langham: BHQ at TF999418; pillbox at TG975421

Ludham: rectangular pillboxes at TG388194 & TG402189

Marham: five assorted pillboxes TF72.10

Matlaske: pillboxes at TG150347 & TG142346

Methwold: two square pillboxes at TL737945, BHQ & LAA gun-pit at TL740930

Oulton Street: octagonal pillbox at TG151278, smaller one at TG142276

Swannington: pillbox at TG121214

Thorpe Abbotts: BHQ at TG190812

Swanton Morley: pillboxes at TG005179, TF996193 & TF993185 + spigot mortar

Watton: pillbox at TF925005

West Raynham: BHQ and seven assorted pillboxes around airfield

Radar site defences

Bard Hill: spigot mortars at TG07.44

Stoke Holy Cross: three pillboxes at TG253024, TG253025 and TG248024

West Beckham: square & hexagonal pillboxes at TG14.38/9

Norwich

TG200111 Hellesdon: pillbox, loop-holed wall and AT rails

TG240083 Norwich: twin Home Guard stores at Thorpe Station

TG275087 Thorpe St Andrew: line of AT blocks alongside railway track

TG273085 Thorpe St Andrew: AT block on track under rail-bridge

TG191082 Earlham: spigot mortar beside B1108 road opposite church

TG195103 New Costessey: rail-block on disused line to Drayton

TG234120 Old Catton: spigot mortar in Park behind houses

TG245068 Trowse: spigot mortar

Kings Lynn

TF603199 West Lynn: two AT blocks + 3 AT rails on bridge

TF626205 Kings Lynn: spigot mortar on Gaywood Road

TF625197 Kings Lynn: 20+ AT rail sockets in front of East Gate, Broad Walk

TF629199 Kings Lynn: spigot mortar alongside railway

Thetford

TL875851 & 873853 Croxton: two pillboxes

TL903868 Kilverstone: pillbox at rail-crossing of A1075 road

TL874825 Nuns Bridge: spigot mortar

TL865834 Thetford Priory: spigot mortar

TL886832 Town Bridge: pillbox with flint camouflage

TL866828 White Hart Lane: spigot mortar

TL876834 Ark PH: Type 28a gun-house converted to infantry role

TL869837 Railway station: pillbox

Diss

TM122824, TM128798 and TM108802: three Type 22 pillboxes

Searchlight site defences

This is a representative sample of the many pillboxes whose existence can only be accounted for by the searchlight site context;

TF618010 Whin Common, Denver

TF618110 Watlington

TG068119 East Tuddenham

TL665924 Poppylots Farm, Feltwell

TG092897 Winfarthing

TG051871 Banham

TF539086 Poppylot Farm, Marshland St James

Other vulnerable points

TF764368 Docking: twin Home Guard stores; 768368: two roofed Norcon pillboxes

TF994131 East Dereham: pillbox at railway level-crossing

TF994162 Hoe: pillbox on railway bridge

TG366920 Ellingham: pillbox on railway bridge [R Waveney Line]

TG10.01 Wymondham: two pillboxes and a spigot mortar at Canwick House

TF975362 Hindringham: type 24 pillbox on T-junction

TF99.33 Thursford: pillbox, loopholes in PH wall, etc at cross-roads

TF66.05 Stradsett: 2 pillboxes, spigot mortars & Home Guard store at cross-roads

TF88.24 East Raynham: three pillboxes around unidentified installation

Chapter 3
Airfields

Watch offices/Control towers

'Fort' type 1959/34: Bircham Newton;

'Fort' type 207/36: Watton, West Raynham [modified to 4698/43]

'Villa' type 2328/39: Horsham St Faith

'Villa' type 5845/39: Swanton Morley

Type 518/40: Shipdham

Type 3156/41 for fighter satellites: Ludham

Type 13726/41 for Bomber satellites: Sculthorpe, Seething, Thorpe Abbotts

Type 12779/41 or 343/43 for all commands: Bodney, Docking, Langham, Little Snoring, Ludham, North Creake, Swannington, Watton,

Type 294/45 for Very Heavy Bombers: Marham, West Raynham

Hangars

Airship hangar, 1917, from Pulham, re-erected at Cardington [Bedfordshire] 1927

Aircraft Repair Shed 164/17: Harling Road

GS Type c1916: Mousehold Heath [Norwich]

Bellman 8349/37: Bircham Newton

Type 'C' 2029/34: Bircham Newton [3], Feltwell [5], Marham [5]

Type 'C' 1978/37: Watton [4], West Raynham [4]

Type 'C' 9181/38: Coltishall [4], Horsham St Faith [5],

Type 'J' 5836/39: Swanton Morley

Type 'B1' MAP 11776/41: North Creake,

Type T2: Fersfield, Foulsham [4], Great Massingham, Little Snoring, Methwold [2], Rackheath, Snetterton Heath, Swanton Morley

Blister hangar: Downham Market, Little Snoring

Hardened Aircraft Shelters [HAS]: Marham

WW2 'E' pen fighter dispersal: Coltishall

Fighter dispersal with blast-walls for Lightnings 4487/53: Coltishall

Domestic buildings

Gymnasium & chapel 15424/41: Great Massingham, Hethel [now museum] & Watton

Gymnasium & cinema 8891/42: Methwold,

Chapel: West Raynham

Gymnasium & Cinema, tb & Nissen 4911/42: North Creake

Squash courts 2078/18: Bircham Newton

Squash court tb 16589/40: Bodney, Great Massingham

NAAFI shop: Coltishall

Institute/Dining-room 1482-4/36: Bircham Newton, Coltishall, Horsham St Faith, Watton

Institute/Dining-room 6848/39: West Raynham

Officers' Mess, timber hutting, Narborough, now West Acre village hall

Sergeants' Mess 3484/36: Bircham Newton

Officers' Mess 2948/34: Bircham Newton, Coltishall, West Raynham

Single Sergeants' Quarters 8378/39: West Raynham

Barrack blocks, 1917, Feltwell

Living huts early 1920s: Bircham Newton

Living huts BCF: Docking, Seething

Barrack block 1100/28: Bircham Newton

Barrack block 2271/34 & 2277/34: Marham

Barrack block 444/36: Watton, West Raynham

Barrack block 2357/36: Bircham Newton

Barrack [H] block 1132/38: Coltishall, West Raynham

Barrack block 11587/38: Bircham Newton

Living huts Nissen 4931/41: Wendling

Barrack block 8/56: Bircham Newton

Pump-house/power-house 694/23 and booster house 1010/23: Bircham Newton

Water-tower & Works Services building 5992/36: Coltishall, West Raynham

Braithwaite tank, single on tower 19-20/41: Bodney, Bylaugh, Great Massingham

Pumphouse tb 291/41: Bodney, Bylaugh

Heating station 9299/38: Coltishall, West Raynham

Training Buildings

25 yard small-arms range 3958/37: Coltishall, West Raynham

Turret trainer 11023/40: North Creake, Snetterton Heath

Link trainer 12386/38: Coltishall

AML Bombing teacher 6301/42: North Creake

Gun turret instructional building 12167/39: Watton, West Raynham

Free gunnery trainer in Blister hangar 7316/42: Great Massingham

Synthetic navigation trainer 2468/42: West Raynham

Dome AA trainer: Langham

Dome trainer for Rapier AA missiles [ADT3]: West Raynham

Flight simulator 1970s: Coltishall

Technical site buildings

Guardroom 166/23: Bircham Newton

Guardroom 494-7/38: Coltishall

Station HQ 1723/36: Bircham Newton, Horsham St Faith

Station HQ with Operations block 1723/36: Coltishall

Operations block 7040/38: Bircham Newton

Station office [Nissen] 12400/41: Attlebridge

Operations block 228/43: Attlebridge, North Pickenham, Seething

Operations block 4891/42: Fersfield

'Uniter' Communications bunker 1980s: Watton

FFMT ready-use shed 3681/36: Bircham Newton, Watton

FFMT ready-use shed 2803/38: West Raynham

Fuel-tanker shed, 4-bay 2773/34: Bircham Newton, Coltishall, Horsham St Faith

Fuel-tanker shed, 6-bay 2773/34: West Raynham

MT office, sheds etc 6225/37 & 778/38: Bircham Newton

MT sheds 6234 + 5907/36: Coltishall, Horsham St Faith, West Raynham

Articulated Trailer Sheds 6879/37 & 7328/38: Coltishall [2], West Raynham [1]

Main workshops [brick] 1354/38: Bircham Newton

Main workshops [concrete] 4923/35: Watton, West Raynham

Main workshops, Romney hutting 5540/42: Fersfield, North Creake

Main workshops, Romney hutting 827/43: Bodney

Main Stores [brick] 7064/37: Bircham Newton

Main stores [concrete] 4287/35: Coltishall, Horsham St Faith, West Raynham

Main Stores, Romney hutting 5852/42: Fersfield, North Creake, Oulton Street

Main Stores, Romney hutting 826/43: Bodney

Fabric store 12773/41: Snetterton Heath

Parachute store 175/36: Bircham Newton, Coltishall

Parachute store 10825/42: North Creake, Rackheath

Dinghy store 2901/43: North Creake

Gas Clothing & Respirator store tb 13730/41: Fersfield

Armoury 7616/37: Bircham Newton, Horsham St Faith, Watton, West Raynham

Armoury 1639/38: Swanton Morley

Norden bomb-sight store 1906 + 3218/43: Attlebridge, North Pickenham

Fusing store [extra heavy bombers] Nissen 7900/42: West Raynham

Inflammables & lubricant store 1967/34: Bircham Newton, Coltishall

Pyrotechnic store 4264/35: West Raynham

Gas Defence Centre 9132/37: Bircham Newton

Gas De-contamination Centre tb 13843/40: Docking

NFE Store 3235/39: West Raynham

NFE/Floodlight tractor + trailer store 12411/41: Rackheath, Swannington [2]

Fire tender shelter, Nissen 12410/41: Rackheath, Swannington, Thorpe Abbotts

Fire tender shed tb 12563/40: Foulsham, Langham

Fire station 4-bay post-WW2: West Raynham

Ambulance garage & mortuary 5703/36: Bircham Newton, Coltishall, West Raynham

Sickbay/decontamination 7503/37: Bircham Newton, Coltishall, Horsham St Faith

Decontamination [unwounded] 6224/37: West Raynham

Stand-by Set house 13241/41: North Creake

Chapter 4 Air defence

AA sites

TG098439 Weybourne: emplacements for 5.25 inch HAA guns at practice camp

TL740930 Methwold airfield: Hexagonal emplacement for 20mm LAA gun

Gorleston-on-Sea, 221 Beccles Road, AA HQ & GOR, former PH, now Vets

Royal Observer Corps posts

TF695319 Dersingham: Orlit A aircraft and underground posts

TG041378 Melton Constable: Orlit A aircraft and underground posts

TF671371 Docking: Orlit B aircraft and underground posts

TM093907 New Buckenham: Orlit B aircraft and underground posts

TM369982 Loddon: Orlit A aircraft post and likely underground post

TG236112 Old Catton, Norwich: ROC semi-sunken protected HQ building

TG392252 Stalham: windmill aircraft post plus underground post

TF856246 West Raynham: aircraft post on WW2 BHQ, plus underground post

TG499197 Winterton-on-Sea: underground post

Bombing decoys either in Norfolk or serving Norfolk airfields

This is a fairly complete list and remains survive at only a few *sites;

Beeston St Lawrence [TG318227] Q for Coltishall

Bramerton [TG305052] Permanent SF, then M[arshalling]/Y[ard]/L[oco]G[lows] [QL] Norwich

Breckles [TL952950] Q for Watton

Burnham Sutton [TF840391] Q for Bircham Newton; Q for Docking

Coxford Heath [TF828307] Q/K for Bircham Newton; Q for Sculthorpe

Crostwick [TG264148] Q for Horsham St Faith

Fulmodestone [TG009306] Q/K for West Raynham; Q for Foulsham

Gately [TF952245] Q for West Raynham

Hempnall [TM256952] Q for Hardwick

Horning [no location] QL Norwich

Lakenheath [TL735814] Q/K for Feltwell

Little Plumstead [TG299121] Permanent SF then M[arshalling]Y[ard]/ F[actory]L[ights] for Boulton & Paul, [QL]

Lound [TM525991] Naval SF/QL for Great Yarmouth

North Creake [TF896392] Q for Docking

North Tuddenham [TG034134] Q/K for Swanton Morley

Salthouse [TG080425] Q for Bircham Newton; Q for Langham

*Sedgeford [TF737363] Q for Bircham Newton

*Snarehill, Thetford [TF896810], Q for Honington

*South Acre [TF796122] Q for Marham; Q for Downham Market

Southery [TL672948] Q for Feltwell

Stanford TL849938 Q for Feltwell

Suffield TG242320] Q for Coltishall

Swaffham [TF832038] Q/K for Marham

Warham St Mary [TF938433] Q for Langham

West Bradenham [TF912070] Q for Watton

Winterton Ness [TG478219] Naval SF/QL for Great Yarmouth

*Wormegay [TF649125] Q for Marham; Q for Downham Market

NB: decoys for Bodney & Snetterton not found; may have been shared with Watton.

Radar sites in World War II

This is a fairly complete list but remains survive at most *sites;

*Stoke Holy Cross [CH] TG252026 [Avenue, monitoring jamming TG296023]

*West Beckham [CH] TG139390 [Kelling, monitoring jamming TG095405]

*Hopton [CHL] TM537991

*Happisburgh [CHL] TG366313

*West Beckham [CHL] TG139390

Hunstanton [CD/CHL TF675419

*Trimingham [CD/CHL] TG290385; Type 9000 Oboe system;

Barrow Common [CD/CHL] TF792433

*Bard Hill [CD/CHL] TG084430

Winterton [CD/CHL] TG499188; Type 9000 Oboe system;

*Happisburgh [temporary CD/CHL] TG375317

Blood Hill [CHEL K series] TG499188 location as Winterton

*Hopton [CHEL K series] TM537991

*Neatishead [GCI] TG347185 & 346188; Type 21 five vehicle system;

Radar sites in the Cold War

*Bawburgh Sector Operations Centre [TG165080] R4 bunker

*Trimingham TG290385 Centimetric Early Warning Station, R1 bunker 1953

*Neatishead TG346184 GCI radar station,

R3 bunker + post-1953 R30 wartime surface operations room; Types 84 & 85 Radars

*Hopton TM540990 CH Extra Low radar station, R2 bunker

*Stoke Holy Cross TG257028 CH radar station

NB: the national Radar Museum and national Radar Archive are at Neatishead, where re-creations of the 1940 Chain Home, the 1942 GCI, and the Cold War early warning systems can all be seen along with equipment and structures from all these three periods.

Barrage balloon sites in Norwich

Site number	location
3	Valpy Avenue school playground
8	Bowthorpe Road school playground
9	29 The Avenue, CEYMS Sports Ground
11	Woodcock/Hunter roads school playground
14	Sprowston Road, field next to City Stadium
15	Valley Drive, Mousehold, common-land
16	Morley Street, children's playground, Kett's Cove
17	City Station, cattle-pen
18	The Close, King Edward VI GS, cricket-ground
20	Thorpe Road, old greyhound track
22	Eaton Park off South Park Avenue
23	Newmarket Road, field south of RASC vehicle-park
25	Lakenham/Hall roads, grazing land at Tuckswood Farm
28	Chapel Field Gardens pavilion
29	Fairfield Road/Town Close, pasture-land
31	City Road, Lakenham cricket-ground
32	Hardy Road, wasteland on bank of River Wensum
34	White Horse Lane, Trowse, field opposite Hospital Farm
36	Crown Point off Whitlingham Lane

Civil Defence

Norwich centrally-controlled Air-raid Sirens:

City Hall City of Norwich School, Eaton Road Co-op Dairy, Fiveways

Water Tower, Quebec Road
Model Senior Girls' School, Dereham Road

Southall's Boot Factory, Cromer Road
Co-op Bakery, Queens Road

Lido Dance-hall, Aylsham Road, Odeon, Botolph Street

Communal air-raid shelter at Thorpe Station

Chapter 5 Logistical support

Barracks, camps & drill halls

Aylsham, Cawston Road, drill hall built during 1930s

Dersingham, Doddshill Road, drill hall built 1930s

East Dereham, First House, Quebec St. mobilisation centre for 5Bn. Norfolk Regt. in 1914; now an Estate Agents' office

Fakenham, Holt Road, drill hall built c1914

Great Yarmouth, Southtown Road, drill hall built during 1930s

Kings Lynn, Wellesley Street, drill hall, opened 1936, for 5Bn. Norfolk Regt.

Kings Lynn, Providence Street, drill hall built 1930s for Norfolk Yeomanry AT unit

Norwich, Britannia Barracks, ITC in WWII; now part of prison

Norwich, 325 Aylsham Road, drill hall of TA HAA artillery unit, built 1939

Stiffkey AA practice camp, now holiday camping-site

Swaffham, Sporle Road, drill hall built 1936 for TA Anti-Tank regiment

Weybourne AA practice camp, now Muckleburgh military collection/museum

Wymondham, Pople Street, drill hall built 1930s for 4Bn. Norfolk Regiment

Depots

Arminghall, Mobilisation Centre, now electronics factory

Ellingham Petrol Depot, now grain storage silos

Fakenham, Mobilisation Centre, now agricultural machinery plant

Hockering, RAF ammunition depot [231 MU]

Pulham, RAF Pyrotechnics and SAA depot [53MU]

Roudham [Harling Road], US Army tank-repair yard, now industrial estate

West Winch, Mobilisation Centre, now refrigerated produce depot

Requisitioned properties [a small selection, see text for more]

Bylaugh Hall, RAF Bomber Command HQ, WWII

Ketteringham Hall [Station 147], USAAF HQ, WWII

Lynford Hall, Mundford, Army HQ, WWI

Catton Hall, Norwich, base for AT unit, then training camp, WWII

Training facilities

TL813967: A1065 roadside memorial to 7th Armoured Division & camps trail

TF70/71 44 Holme: blockhouses associated with tank-gunnery training

TL901814 Snarehill: bombing-range Quadrant Tower

Snettisham: USAAF anti-aircraft gunnery training camp

STANTA Stanford Battle Area between Thetford and Watton

Stiffkey Camp [AA training]

Titchwell Marshes, tank-gunnery range

Weybourne AA practice camp

Prisoner-of-War Camps in Norfolk World War I

Kenninghall [Uphall & East Harling]; Whitwell; Thetford [Warren Wood & Croxton]

Kings Lynn [St James's Hall, Estuary Road, & Lynn Recreation Ground

Norwich [Aldborough, Thorpe Norfolk War Hospital & Lakenham Mills]

Snettisham, Wereham, North Elmham, Gressenhall, Docking, Houghton, Gayton;

Burnham Market [Maltings & Burnham Norton]

World War II

Botesdale [No 56], Uplands Camp [No 131] and Redgrave Park military hospital [No 231] all ascribed to Diss but actually in Suffolk

Hampton Green, Fakenham [No 82]

Kimberley Park [No 132]

Wolterton Camp, Aylsham [No 409]

North Lynn Farm, Kings Lynn [No 280]

Snettisham RAF Camp [No 255]

Mousehold Heath Camp [No 253]

Hospitals [a small selection, see text for more]

World War I

Norfolk War Hospital, Thorpe, Norwich

World War II

Redgrave Hall, USAAF hospital and associated PoW Camp 231 in Suffolk

Wymondham, Emergency Medical Service hospital, used by USAAF

BIBLIOGRAPHY

DOCUMENTS IN TNA:

WO 166/329,464,468 & 625; WO 199/2500: papers of 11 Corps, 1940-1

ANON:
Thetford/Snarehill [Norfolk]; in Airfield Review 116, Sept. 2007, Thetford

BALFOUR, G:
The Armoured Train; 1981, London

BANGER, J:
Norwich at War; 1974, Norwich

BIRD, C:
The Fixed Defences of North & East Norfolk in the two World Wars: a modern survey part I: 1991, Jnl. of Norfolk Industrial Archaeology Soc. Vol 5 No. 1

BIRD, C:
The Fixed Defences of North & East Norfolk in the two World Wars: a modern survey part II: 1992, Jnl. of Norfolk Industrial Archaeology Soc. Vol 5 No. 2

BIRD, C:
Norfolk's Fixed Defences in the two World Wars: a sequel: 1995, Jnl. of Norfolk Industrial Archaeology Soc. Vol 5 No. 5

BIRD, C:
Silent Sentinels; Norfolk's 20th century defences; 1999, Dereham, Larks Press

BOWMAN, MW:
Echoes of East Anglia: 2006, Tiverton

BOWYER, M:
Action Stations 1: East Anglia; 1979 & 1990, Wellingborough, PSL

BOWYER, M:
Action Stations Revisited, No 1 Eastern England; 2000, Manchester

CHRISTOPHER, J:
Balloons at War; 2004, Stroud

COCROFT, WD:
Bard Hill survey report; 1998, EH/RCHME, Cambridge

COCROFT, WD:
RAF Trimingham survey report; 1998, EH/RCHME, Cambridge

COCROFT, WD & THOMAS, RJC:
Cold War, Building for Nuclear Confrontation 1946-1989; 2003, English Heritage, Swindon

DAVIES, KM:
The Observer in the Royal Navy 1908-2003; 2005, Darlington

DELVE, K:
Military Airfields of East Anglia; 2005, Ramsbury

DOBINSON, C:
Twentieth Century Fortifications in England Volume II Anti-invasion defences of WWII; 1996, York, CBA

DOBINSON, C:
Twentieth Century Fortifications in England Volumes VII.1 [Text] and VII. 2 [Appendices] Acoustics & Radar; 2000, York, CBA

DOBINSON, C:
Twentieth Century Fortifications in England Volumes VI.1 [Text] and VI. 2 [Appendices] Coastal Artillery, 1900-56; 2000, York, CBA

DOBINSON, C:
Fields of Deception, bombing decoys in WWII; 2000, London

DOBINSON, C:
AA Command; 2001, London

DOYLE, P:
Thetford [Snarehill]; in Airfield Review 75; June 1997, Ware

FAIRHEAD, H:
Decoy Sites, wartime deception in Norfolk & Suffolk; nd, Flixton

FERGUSON, A:
Death of an Airfield- RAF Coltishall; in Airfield Review 113, December 2006, Thetford

FOOT, W:
Beaches, fields, streets and hills; 2006, York, CBA

FORTY, G:
7th Armoured Division; 2003, Hersham, Ian Allan

FOYNES, JP:
The Battle of the East Coast 1939-45; 1994, privately printed

GORE, LL:
The History of Hunstanton; 1983, Bognor Regis

GREHAN, J:
Outward Bound; June 2008, Storrington, Britain at War 14

HOARE, A:
Standing up to Hitler [Norfolk Home Guard]; 1997, Wymondham

JOHNSON, B:
The Secret War; 1978, London, BBC

KENT, P:
Fortifications of East Anglia: 1988, Lavenham

KENT, P:
The Fixed Defences; in Gliddon, G [ed] Norfolk & Suffolk in the Great War; 1988, Norwich

KENT, P:
East Anglian fortifications in the 20th Century; in Fortress 3; 1989, Liphook

KING, G: Notes on the history of the Pulham Air Station; in Airfield Review 116, September 2007, Thetford

KINSEY, G:
Pulham Pigs; 1988, Lavenham

KINSEY, G:
Boulton & Paul Aircraft; 1992, Lavenham

MCCAMLEY, N:
Cold War Secret Nuclear Bunkers; 2002, Barnsley

MCCAMLEY, N:
Disasters Underground; 2004, Barnsley

MACKSEY, K:
Armoured Crusader; [biography of Sir Percy Hobart]; 2004, London

MEERES, F:
Norfolk in the First World War; 2004, Chichester

MINISTRY OF INFORMATION:
Land at War; 1945, reprinted 2001, HMSO, Norwich

NARBOROUGH ARG:
The Great Government Airfield; 2000, Narborough

OSBORN, M & TOWLER, R:
The short, but unusual career of RAF Fersfield; Airfield Review 86; April 2000, Stockport

OSBORNE, M:
Defending Britain; 2004, Stroud

OSBORNE, M:
Always Ready, the drill halls of Britain's volunteer forces; 2006, Leigh-on-Sea

OSBORNE, M:
Pillboxes in Britain and Ireland; 2008, Stroud

RAWLINSON, A:
The Defence of London; 1923, London

STOREY, N:
Norfolk at War; 1995, Stroud

STOREY, N:
Norfolk at Work; 1997, Stroud

SIMMONS, G:
RFC Harling Road; in Airfield Review 95; July 2002, Thetford

SOCKETT, EW:
Stockton-on-Tees Y Station: in Fortress 8; February 1991, Liphook

TAYLOR, B:
West Raynham-A final [and very personal reflection]; in Airfield Review 110, April 2006, Thetford

THOMAS, RJC:
RAF West Raynham; in Airfield Review 102 & 103; October & December 2001, Stockport

TOWLER, R & OSBORN, M:
The history of RAF Feltwell & RAF Methwold: in Airfield Review 83; July 1999, & 84, October, 1999, Stockport

WARLOW, LT CDR B:
Shore Establishments of the Royal Navy; 1992 & 2000, Liskeard

WILLIAMSON, T:
England's Landscapes: East Anglia; 2006, London, EH

WILLS, H:
Pillboxes, a study of UK defences 1940; 1985, London

WOOD, D:
Attack Warning Red; the ROC 1925-1992; 1976 & 1992, Portsmouth

WYNN, H:
RAF Nuclear Deterrent Forces 1946-69; 1994, HMSO, London

Useful Websites

www.britarch.ac.uk/projects/dob
[Defence of Britain Project data]

www.pillbox-study-group.org.uk
[Pillbox Study Group]

www.airfield-research-group.co.uk
[Airfield Research Group]

www.info@pillboxesuk.com
[Ian Sanders]

NORFOLK INDEX

Notes: page numbers expressed thus: ***40***, represent illustrations; all Army, Navy & Air Force etc entries may be found under "Units";

U

W

Y

Z